FINDING TIME
FOR YOUR SELF

FINDING TIME FOR YOUR SELF

A Spiritual Survivor's Workbook

52 weeks of reflections
and exercises for busy people

PATTY DE LLOSA

sussex
ACADEMIC
PRESS
Brighton • Chicago • Toronto

2 4 6 8 10 9 7 5 3 1

First published in 2015 by
SUSSEX ACADEMIC PRESS
PO Box 139
Eastbourne BN24 9BP

and in the United States of America by
SUSSEX ACADEMIC PRESS
Independent Publishers Group
814 N. Franklin Street, Chicago, IL 60610

and in Canada by
SUSSEX ACADEMIC PRESS (CANADA)
24 Ranee Avenue, Toronto, Ontario M6A 1M6

British Library Cataloguing in Publication Data
A CIP catalogue record for this book is available from the British Library.

Library of Congress Cataloging-in-Publication Data
Llosa, Patty de.
Finding time for your self : a spiritual survivor's workbook : 52 weeks of reflections and exercises for busy people / Patty de Llosa.
pages   cm
Includes bibliographical references and index.
ISBN 978-1-84519-671-4 (pbk : alk. paper)
1. Spiritual life. 2. Self-help techniques. I. Title.
BL624.L6196 2015
204'.4—dc23

2014046810

Typeset & designed by Sussex Academic Press, Brighton & Eastbourne.
Printed by Edwards Brothers Malloy, AnnArbor, MI

Contents

⌄

CONTENTS

Acknowledgments

This book owes much thanks to Canadian litterateur John Robert Colombo, who came up with the original idea of a spiritual survivor's workbook when I sent him some blogs I had written. Many thanks also to editor Tony Grahame at Sussex Academic Press, who offered to publish it and held my hand through the process. Blessings on you both!

The bibliography that follows represents a small listing of the thousand minds and hearts who have shared their wisdom, whether via mainstream religions, Gurdjieffian, Jungian, Taoist or Alexander studies, or brilliant contemporary mind/body science. All have fed me richly — body, soul and spirit, for which I'm truly grateful.

As always, my best support has been my immediate family, parents who held up a mighty mirror of dedication to duty, truth, and love, and three adult children who have shared many of my adventures and taught me a lot of what I know.

Finally, the truest spiritual education is extended from person to person—an experiential wisdom heartfully shared by living the teaching together. And in that regard I have been very lucky. First my mother, Louse Welch, then Jeanne de Salzmann, Pauline de Dampierre, Marion Woodman, and Peter Brook have held up to me, by their very presence-in-action, a mirror to the high possibility of being human. I had no choice but to attempt to live the teaching they represent as best I could, and in the process have learned to listen to my own inner guide, the Lord of the Heart.

Introduction

Most of us feel scattered much of the time. Like the dismembered Egyptian god Osiris, we are spread out all over our personal world. *Finding Time* offers help to bring you back together again and learn how to re-member yourself, not by withdrawing from the world but staying right in the middle of the action.

Fifty-two thought-provoking reflections on questions raised by daily life are followed by practical exercises that will help you stay inwardly alive and present to meet life's many challenges. The meditations offer a path to inner peace as they invite you to pause and reflect for a few minutes each day, while the practical exercises engage you in day-by-day experiences as you seek a more balanced sense of yourself in the midst of outer activity. You can start at the beginning and go through to the end of the book, or select the theme for each week that most touches the heart of your particular situation.

Remember the old Shaker song "It's a gift to be simple"? The lyrics express the solution as 'turning', until "by turning, turning we come round right." When I turn away for a short time from my activities, goals and commitments and toward my inner Self, I discover a world that's just as active and full of surprises as the outer one that draws me into physical and mental action. As I turn my attention to the world within, I reconnect with the person I essentially am, in the depths of my being.

You may well ask: "How do I find time for an inner life when I'm too busy even to think about it?" Well, the art of living deeply depends on learning to turn at those difficult moments, in the midst of our busy lives. What's more, you will discover that as we re-connect with our inner rhythms, we will find true renewal and repose.

The stakes have never been higher in this increasingly dangerous world, full of unknown forces that act on us in unexpected ways: a faltering economy, dread of terrorism, increasing anxiety about our jobs, our family, our future. The word 'stress' is on everyone's lips, and we can't make it go away. It's hardwired into our nervous system. However, we can learn to manage stress before it turns into *distress*.

For that, a new attitude is necessary. Life insists on our participation and affirms us in many different ways, but as we hurry through our days trying to keep up with its many demands, we are starved for attention to our own presence, our sense of being here and now. As ancient Celtic tradition has it, expressed in the words of John O'Donohue, "If we become addicted to the external, our interiority will haunt us. We will become hungry with a hunger no image, person, or deed can still . . . In order to keep our balance, we need to hold the interior and exterior, visible and invisible, known and unknown, temporal and eternal, ancient and new, together."

Finding Time offers a path to this holding of interior and exterior together, inviting a richer participation in daily activities. And as soon as we turn toward our inner being, help to maintain a sense of presence becomes miraculously available — it is "nearer to us than breathing," according to the Hindu philosopher Shankara. Fresh energy rises within us when we meet life's demands from a new point of view, joining the multitude of fellow seekers, past and present, who have become Spiritual Survivors.

My own story: I fought for balance in a constantly changing world, first as a reporter for *Time*, then married to a Peruvian, raising a family and founding a United Nations pre-school in a foreign country. When my marriage collapsed and I came back to New York after twenty years in Peru, I turned again to journalism to support my family — as managing editor of *American Fabrics & Fashions*, then associate editor of *Leisure*, and finally deputy chief of reporters of *Fortune*. The pace of my life never ceased to demand all I could give as a single mother of three, dependent on skill and ingenuity to keep the family afloat.

Despite this endlessly shifting kaleidoscope of personal and professional duty, my daily life was often interrupted by a deep inner call — a summons to another kind of action. Like all of us, I am a citizen of two worlds, continually summoned in two seemingly opposed directions: toward the inner and the outer life. Usually we attend to the louder (outer) one because the other call, that still, small inner voice, is not so easy to hear. We need to learn how to tune ourselves to its vibration, with the generous guidance available to us from those who have gone before.

I was lucky. Born into a family of seekers gathered around G. I. Gurdjieff, I was grounded by his "Work in Life" teaching from an early age. I was also stirred and solaced by many spiritual messages. A religious Christian in childhood, I later pursued the writings of Hinduism, Buddhism, Judaism, Taoism and Zen with equal zeal. At 30, I met Tai Chi master T. T. Liang and soon began to teach under his orders. In mid-life, guilt-ridden and devastated by the breakup of my family, I delved into the work of C. G. Jung, which led to the writing of my second book, *Taming Your Inner Tyrant*. When I retired from *Fortune*, I signed up for the three-year training to teach F. M. Alexander's neuromuscular re-education technique. (For more about all these studies, see my first book, *The Practice of Presence: Five Paths for Daily Life*, Morning Light Press, 2006.)

I cannot claim that all my questions were answered by my years of seeking. On the contrary, as you join me in this endeavor, I hope you will find that your questions are intensified. And that, over time, you'll realize, as I did, that the questions are nourishment enough. To live a more abundant life we must ask our questions again and again. Answers will not bring us closer to our heart's desire; we need better questions.

As you undertake this exploration, you'll discover that, along with all our 'doing,' this return to oneself becomes an active, joyous experience. The aim is neither to disappear into a subjective world nor to lose contact with ourselves as we engage in outer life. Rather, we strive to embrace our deeper self, to listen to our soul's call as we meet the world's demands and distractions. That call is always unexpected and immediate. It may last only a heartbeat, but it transforms our daily lives.

Being and Doing

There seem to be two ends to the spectrum we call life — two polar opposites, two extremes. I think of them as Being and Doing. If I wish to be present, I must turn my attention toward myself, to my thoughts, my reactions, my sensations, and answer with my whole self the question: Who am I? But if I wish to write the Great American Novel, to convince a prospective client that I have the best product, or simply to check items off my to-do list, I must turn away from myself and focus my energy outside, to express, convince, accomplish.

I've noticed that when I sit quietly, moved by the glory of a sunset over the sea, my world stands still. I am at peace. But as soon as I stand up and go inside to prepare dinner, the calm and clarity vanish. "Is that inevitable?" I ask. While these two opposite modes never seem to co-exist, there's an inexplicable statement from the Gospel According to Thomas, that "I am a movement and a rest." Does that mean there's hope that the two will converge so that I can do and be at the same time?

Although I suspect most of us lose our connection with ourselves as soon as we go into movement, great dancers, great athletes and great actors are visibly centered. As we watch them move, we can't help but see how deeply connected they are with themselves while giving a superlative performance. What's their secret?

Clearly it has something to do with attention. When I'm sitting here quietly, my attention, which usually pours out into my life, into the things and people around me, comes to rest in me. Here I am. So why does it disappear when I move?

I've heard about the effortless effort, the un-aimed arrow which the blindfolded Zen archer unleashes from his bow in a centered and relaxed state. Zing! It cleaves the bullseye. How could that apply to me? Is it telling me that I'm bow, arrow and target all at once?

Excuse me! There are a million things to do: meals to cook; money to make; people to be cared for. Even a Zen monk needs a roof over his head, clothes on his body, and food in his bowl. How does that happen if I'm not up and doing? So here I am, either running on a treadmill, adrift on the sea of life, or sinking deep into metaphysics. That's a quicksand I'll try to avoid if at all possible, but I want to understand how two seeming opposites can come together, so I will have to open the door to larger rooms in my mind. I hope you will join me.

To open those doors, we need to ask questions of ourselves and undertake experiments in Being. Begin today. As the wise folk like to say, it's the only day you have. Get a special notebook so you can write down your perceptions on this new journey of discovery that begins . . . right now.

Day 1
This week try to notice how these two modes, Being and Doing, play through you during the day. It helps to name them — "Ah, this is me, Doing." Or to realize when you sit down for a moment with a cup of coffee that it's an opportunity for Being with your Self. When do you live in one mode and when in the other? When does one of them seem more nurturing? Which makes you feel better? It often it feels so good to move or to get things done — so no judgments, please. Just observations.

Day 2
After a day of naming, make the experiment for one day of giving a little more time to Being. What does that mean? How to try? Meditation is an obvious choice, but walking in the park is another. And if you are stuck on the job, you can listen to the sounds of the world from deeper inside. Try tuning in to the vibrations of the voices in a crowded room. Speak your heart with a true friend. Give someone at the office the gift of your presence. Right at your desk you can call a friend on the phone or pay a visit in your mind to someone you love.

Day 3
You'll find many other ways once you get started. Begin to make a list. Think of it like this: if 90% of our waking hours are spent in the doing mode — putting out energy on the job, the laundry or the internet —

when will there be time for rest and restorative reflection? Schedule into your daybook a few times you'd like to try to stop for a moment of reflection. A ten-minute pause that refreshes the spirit would probably help you perform better at whatever you have to do today.

Day 4

You might take a moment today to think about some of your family members, living or dead. Call up memories of someone's way of being or invite an image of their face to enter your inner space. Stay and sit with them for a few minutes. What feelings do they awaken in you? What memories do you begin to recall that you'd almost forgotten? Begin to notice that whenever you give space for a moment of Being, you become more aware of your feelings.

Day 5

*Choose to read something nourishing or thought-provoking every day this week for 15 minutes. Listen to music as if it were playing deep inside you. Next time you sit down for a coffee break, listen to what's going on within you — whether symphony or cacophony. We're all members of a species called human **beings**, not human "**doings**." There are many things happening all the time deep within us that we are almost never aware of.*

Who Am I?

A perennial question that has never had a satisfactory answer. However, reminding myself to think about it provokes reflection, which can send me in search of the meaning of my life.

There's a lot we know about ourselves. For example, there's a small child within each of us who loves, hates and struggles to succeed. She loves to be alone looking at the stars or listening to the sounds of the sea, to dance and sing, to be startled into laughter by the call of a bird or rejoice in the discovery of a blooming flower.

There's a clue! A child loves surprises. As I advance through my day with to-do list in hand, determined to get my stuff done, I can break away from habitual patterns and move to another level of awareness that links me to the conscious experience of the present moment. How can I awaken to such a possibility?

Oughts, musts and shoulds could be a key. Will I look upon them differently if I discover my true identity? Perhaps a new kind of duty will reveal itself — a duty to *be present to my life*. That recently discovered child inside needs room to grow, to express herself. She invites me to dance, to sing, to listen, to learn, to wonder. Hiding in all of us, even at the last stages of life, she brings joy to whoever gives her room to breathe.

So what about the adult in each of us? Mine tries to figure out everything that's going to happen as far ahead of time as possible, so she can meet every contingency with her best defenses in place. In dialogues with my inner personas I called her Mrs. Rigid (see Chapter Three of *The Practice of Presence*). "No time out until your job is done, even for a walk on the beach!" I disliked her intensely until I discovered to my astonishment that she was rigid because she was afraid.

Fear of what? Here's where it gets interesting. The child *wants* surprises but Mrs. Rigid fears them. One is open, curious, wants to explore; the other wants "nothing new, thank you!" Mrs. Rigid is in cahoots with my thinking machine, which is always turned on to "what I ought to do," or "OMG, what if that happened?"

I ask myself, "Who am I *now*?" and discover someone who wishes to be awake to life's possibilities and difficulties, in the spirit of that youthful freshness within all of us. She longs to respond with an open heart to the tasks and situations that confront us every day.

When you decide to explore the question "Who am I?" gear up your courage to meet parts of yourself you didn't suspect were there. Be ready for surprises as you observe different kinds of reactions in yourself. As Rumi says, "Within us are many things. There is mouse in us, and there is bird. The bird carries the cage upwards, while the mouse drags it down. A hundred thousand different wild beasts are together within us, but they are all converging on that moment when the mouse will renounce its mousehood and the bird its birdhood, and all become one." That's why, when we turn within, we discover inner opinions that don't necessarily agree with each other or with who we think we are.

Day 1
Begin today to explore the many inner voices of which you may seldom be aware. As you listen to them today, write their opinions down. Perhaps you, too, have a child inside; a Mr. or Mrs. Rigid who likes things one way and no other; a rebel without a cause. These personality fragments live in us like a cast of characters who appear in certain situations and offer a variety of responses to the daily situations and people you encounter. You'd do well to get to know them.

Day 2
Once you have discovered one of them, try giving that persona a name. Today, begin to build up your own personal Cast of Characters. List them in your new notebook and explore what any of them wants from you.

Day 3
Today try to catch the resonance, the different tone of voice of each persona, as well as its distinct attitude toward you and toward life. Engage in a dialogue with a few of them, as I did in Taming Your Inner Tyrant. *Listen carefully to what they say, but remember that no individual voice represents the whole of you.*

Day 4
Do you have a black-robed Judge, like mine, who criticizes and passes judgment on your every move? (When I don't follow his orders he'll see that I suffer for what he considers my mistakes.) If you do, notice when he criticizes you today and write down his comments. Maybe you thought, as I did, that he was the voice of your conscience, but he's not. He's just the keeper of the rules you've been living by — rules probably forced on you by accident or childhood situations. What rules are they?

Day 5
Once you've written down some of the rules your personal judge wants you to live by, ask yourself, "Why do I choose to follow them?" Experiment with them today. Maybe some are good ones, but do you accept them because you feel it is right to do so? Ask yourself often Baba Yaga's question in the Russian fairytale: Are you following your rules "of your own free will or by compulsion?" (For more on this, see Marion Woodman and Robert Bly's The Maiden King.*) As you discover that none of these inner characters is "you," you are left again with the question: "Who am I?"*

Surprised by Love

The things I love are important, no matter how inconsequential they may appear to the rational mind. Whether it be a flower, a silken skirt or my own true partner, what I love introduces me to myself. It may be a 'me' I don't know well or have paid little attention to. Whether it's a tiny corner or even a huge part of me, I need to know it better. Whatever I love needs to be appreciated because it is nourishment for the heart.

Then why do I turn away so often? How many times have I begun to pause and shift into a quieter mode because I was touched by something I saw or heard or felt. But then I'd mutter, "No time for this!" and push on to the next task without giving the present inner experience its due. Yes, it's important to be on time, to deliver the goods, to keep one's word (and one's job!), but don't make the mistake I made for so many years. Don't move on too quickly, away from that brief moment of recognition, of inner communication with a gentler aspect of yourself.

There are all kinds of reasons to move away from the taste of love. Perhaps I'm not prepared for it. I'm taken by surprise and can't digest this new message. Sometimes there's just too much on my plate and I fear an emotional train wreck if I open myself to something new. So I switch back into what I'm ready for. Marion Woodman spoke to all of us when she said: "The fear of receiving resonates in the deepest levels of the psyche. To receive is to let life happen, to open to grief and loss, to open to love and delight."

When I open to what touches me — whether it's a flower, a personal exchange, a gift given or received — it lives on in me. It lights a hungry, dark corner inside that needs these moments much as a seed needs water. Such precious moments should never be glossed over quickly. Here I am, here where I love, here where I recognize an affinity I may not understand. It is here that new connections are forged, even if just for a glancing moment.

At such times I need to pause and recognize the value of what has broken through my inner defenses. Where did it come from and what inspired it? I love. I am nourished. Why was I so passive to it?

Personally, I love words. I delight in discovering the perfect phrase to clarify what I'm trying to say. I also love a good joke, although I seldom remember them long enough to pass them on. I love to laugh, but how many laughs have I stifled? I love to dance but how many times have I held my body still? I love to sing but how many songs have died on my lips?

As we grow up, we inevitably turn our backs on many pleasures. And there's a reason for it. School and college studies take up our time. Then finding and keeping a job, raising a family or becoming part of a social circle where we can function and serve. All this adds up to saying "no" to some things because we choose to say "yes" to others. But now is the time to rediscover some of those simple pleasures, to treasure what we love and welcome it even when we're busy.

The ancient Celtic tradition, interpreted for us by John O'Donohue, celebrates Anam Cara (Gaelic for "soul friend") — love of the friend within, love of your Self. "The soul needs love as the body needs air," he writes. "In the warmth of love, the soul can be itself. All the possibilities of your human destiny are asleep in your soul. You are here to realize and honor those possibilities. When love comes into your life, unrecognized dimensions of your destiny awaken and blossom and grow . . . Love is the threshold where divine and human presence ebb and flow into each other."

Day 1
If an unexpected emotion transfixes you, try not to move away from it too quickly, even though the horses of desire or duty are already pulling at the reins. It may be as inconsequential as delight in the sunlight on your face, or as meaningful as the touch of a beloved hand. Why not stop a moment to take it in? Why not take the time to slip it into the pocket of your heart, the way a child squirrels away a pretty stone? Savor such moments a little longer today.

Day 2

Start today by asking, "What do I really like?" Make a list of your favorite things and activities as you prepare for the day. Then find out whether you can make time for any of them. Does what's on your list still attract you in the heat of the action? At the end of the day, write your discoveries down. It would also be useful to write down what turns you off, annoys you, or makes you really angry.

Day 3

Pay attention today to any tentative beginnings of joy or pleasure that may surge up from nowhere. Your recognition of them may be fleeting, but stay there long enough to take them in. Don't cut them short. And if you catch yourself rushing away in denial, recognize that you are face to face with an emotional habit. "Why did I say 'no' so fast?" Register the fact and try to be more alert next time. Ask yourself, "Why do I cut myself off when emotion rises from an unknown source?" Choose to live more deeply.

Day 4

Once you've decided to explore this uncharted territory, go in search of less familiar likes and dislikes. Pay attention to what different parts of yourself like or dislike. Travel below your everyday habits, below the mind's approval, below the rules you've set for yourself in a challenging world. Believe it or not, there's someone unknown in each us, a person we sometimes glimpse for a moment or perhaps have never met. Write down your discoveries.

Day 5

Exchanges with others are very important. The smile on someone's face might make you smile back before you remember you don't know or don't like this person. The sound of a song, the swish of a skirt, the smell of a flower, a muffin, or a perfume can take you to a place once known but long gone. Spend a moment with it. Write about it. You are gathering precious treasures, mining for gold. And if you pay attention to these special moments of discovery, they will happen more often. Cherish them. They are telling you who you are; both the person you think you are and the person in yourself you may not know at all!

Crooked Things

It's time to celebrate crooked things. We often seek perfection but will we ever get it all straight? I don't think so. Maybe we once believed that "straight is the gate and narrow is the way" and went in search of it. But by now most of us are pretty sure we're not going to find it. And even if we did manage to squeeze through that narrow aperture from time to time, didn't our path become pretty crooked from then on? How often do we stray from our intention out of curiosity or stupor or to smell the roses!

Nature moves in curves and curlicues. Perhaps that's why I love the many crooked trees even more than the few arrow-straight ones. They look like they've fought for survival in a tough world. Like me. Like you. Notice how they grow both up and sideways, twisted and curved from battling the wind, the storms, or a gardener's pruning sheers.

And how about those gnarly bushes I passed the other day on the road through the park? Balanced on top of a huge rock, their roots twisted every which way down its side to sink deep into a narrow crevasse at the bottom. How I admire the struggle of those roots down the rocky slope, actively in search of earth so they can nourish themselves, while their branches reach toward heaven, stretching up to the sun.

Every time I see crooked roots and branches, they rivet my attention. Static, yet dynamic, fixed but moving every which way, they tell their life story. Their presence is a history book, just like ours. They grow upwards, yes, always up, but to the sides as well. "That's me," I acknowledge as I pass. "Maybe that's all of us."

We reach upward, trying to better ourselves and our conditions in many ways, seeking nourishment from the sun but often forced to move to one side or another just to survive. We are shaped by our longings, by the facts of our lives, and by the force of the elements. Including our own elemental desires.

As an incorrigible perfectionist, I often get annoyed at myself for falling short. Unfortunately I also apply the same standard to other people. That's just not fair! Inevitably, everyone falls short. What an amazing world it would be if we were all perfect! But it's not real. What we think of as perfect may be simply our own opinion. Our perfect world is often based on personal attitudes we've gathered during a lifetime of comings and goings.

Day 1
Does a secret desire to be perfect lurk half-submerged in your unconscious? If so, you're like me. I'll bet even when you succeed you're often disappointed. What are your "upward" aims? Write them down. How many of your big plans succeeded? What was the cost of success when they did? What did you accuse yourself of if you failed? Put it all down on paper so you can review it later and see if you still agree with it.

Day 2
It's hard to give up the habit of our judgmental attitudes, but if we could, we might be able to forgive ourselves and everyone else for being human. Believe it or not, everyone's in trouble on this one, not just you and me! We've all been brought up under constant pressure to judge, to compete, and to succeed. But in order to find real understanding, more time is needed to investigate both sides of any problem. Notice and write down any of your judgments about other people and your habitual attitudes toward them, as well as how you criticize your own performance.

Day 3
Engage actively in questioning yourself with an alert mind and heart. Every evening you could weigh each judgment you made during the day in the balance of your quiet mind. To do that, you must put aside your first reaction, whatever it may be, and think the situation over. Whenever you suspect you've satisfied yourself too quickly, affirming only one side of the scales of justice, call it habit rather than reasoning, and return to contemplate the other side. At first it may not be easy to discriminate between critical thinking and judgmental attitudes. Start by noticing how annoyed you are at yourself. When you criticize your performance say, "Wait a minute. I want to be me, not some genius,

some perfect Doer." Then apply the same criteria when you're criticizing someone else. If you do this honorably, you'll gather a lot of useful, Who-am-I? information in your notebook.

Day 4
From early childhood on, we've been influenced by a lot of opinions. We collect them, often automatically, stuff them in the closet of our mind, and bring them out whenever they seem appropriate or when we need a quick point of view to win an argument. Can you separate your principles from your opinions? Make one list for the principles, another for the borrowed opinions. Can you figure out where they originally came from?

Day 5
Why is it so important to study and weigh our criticisms? Because while it's natural to want to be different or do things better, we often move away from being who we truly are in our efforts to succeed. Tell yourself out loud, "Yes, maybe there's a better way but I'm doing my best, here, on my crooked path. I accept who I am and I'll try again." Give up, at least for today, insisting how things OUGHT to be and embrace how they are. And how you are. That's where real life is!

Yesterday's Gone!

I'm haunted by a song I heard this morning in the subway, belted out by a black woman with a voice like an organ. "YESTERDAY'S GONE," she sang, her voice resonating throughout the tunnel. Then, more quietly and with some sadness, "Tomorrow may never be mine."

That moment was powerful, but it wasn't new. We've all heard that it's better to live in the Now. However, personal experience has taught us that this place between yesterday and tomorrow can sometimes be very painful. Yesterday provided us with lots of living, along with all the frustration, the striving, the urging on and satisfying of desires. And the thought of tomorrow gives us the impetus to get up today and go to work. It's for something, we assume, not just for now but for some future goal, some better situation, or even simply to have enough to eat, that we drive ourselves to accomplish what's got to be done today.

But what about today, all by itself? If I'm happy, it's fine. All is well. When I'm feeling good I can relish today, embrace it like a lover. But what if I'm aching in body and spirit, if nothing can solace the pain, even as I tell myself I have to get on with my life?

Yesterday's injuries are dulled and hopefully healing. But today may contain raw anguish for which there seems to be no cure. For example, the death of parents is major, and one of mine died recently, while the other lives on in need of my continuing care. How I long to be with the person she once was! So I sometimes secretly wish not to be where I am when I'm with her, then hate myself for how I feel. At such times, I try to drown "today" in forgetting, by working or reading or eating or distracting myself in some way from this place of pain.

Mired in such a state, I would welcome the dulling of memory and sensation so that my suffering could fade into the foggy past, or become fertilizer for a new, hopefully happier future. But "now" can color that future so it seems like an empty desert where the sun beats down uncaring, and unforgiving winds blow sand in my eyes. With that thought I begin to weep. Somehow that helps. Perhaps there may be a way out of this place. And that booming voice suggests an interim solution:

"Lord for my sake
Teach me to take
One day at a time."

Some of us carry a lot of yesterday with us. It weighs us down. An old soldier told Gurdjieff how he had suffered all his life from an incident in World War I in which he had carried a wounded buddy away from the front lines on his back, hoping to save him. But, instead, his friend's body had served as a shield, and when they arrived at the medical station, he discovered his friend was riddled with the bullets aimed at him. "Accept it like your skin," said Gurdjieff, with a deeply compassionate look. You may or may not have your own bullet-ridden bodies on your back, but we all carry guilt and suffering, sometimes difficult to bear. Accept it as an aspect of the unique, wounded human being that you are, that we all are.

Day 1
When you feel sad or anxious, make this experiment for a short while during the day: try to come into the present moment, whatever that may mean to you. Try to accept whatever's going on in you, as you ask yourself how you feel right now and attempt to formulate an accurate answer, down to the last detail. Don't be afraid to weep. Tears can heal.

Day 2
Another day, notice how often you call up past memories, or even relive moments you lived through only an hour or two before. Listen to how you talk to yourself. We often tell ourselves: "I should have said or done this"; or "I wish something different had happened." Write down all those internal mutterings.

Day 3
The following day, notice what you accuse yourself of. We often attack ourselves for being unsatisfactory. But who's the judge of that? Guilt

about past actions serves no purpose. It's indigestible and only weighs you down. Yes, you want to meet the present moment with your best effort. Did you try your best? Okay, maybe you didn't. Now accept that as a fact rather than an accusation, and determine to try more sensitively next time.

Day 4
Notice today how often you worry about what hasn't yet happened or set up a situation in your mind that may never come about. How much time in your day do you feel anxious? Make notes to remind yourself when and why. In the evening, look back to what actually took place. Was that energy spent on anxiety worth the candle? If not, try to blow that particular candle out.

Day 5
Finally, as you become aware of how often you spend time with your mind focused either on the past or on the future, set your findings down in two columns. Which is longer, past or future? Wonder to yourself why this is so, and whether where you are currently focused feeds the soul. No matter whether past or future called you most, the fact is that today is all we have. Tomorrow may never be ours. Now is the only reality.

Conduct Your Blooming

"Conduct your blooming . . . in the noise and whip of the whirlwind."
Strange message in a stranger place. I don't know who said it, but
this statement suddenly appeared on a huge wall in the 59th St.
subway tunnel that connects the Lexington Avenue trains to the
N and R lines. For many months the wall had been roped off and
covered over with brown paper: reconstruction in progress. What
else can you expect in New York City, where everything's always
under construction!

Then one fine day the plastic barrier was cut and the paper pulled
down. There it was, gleaming in vivid colors, a giant mosaic
mural with a great scroll of a message that ran in a wavy line up
and down from ceiling to floor and back again.

Who would expect to find such an uplifting message underground! Yet those of us who travel by subway every day have got
used to hearing Bach or Segovia or music from the Andes, played
on diverse instruments that compete with the noise of the trains
as they come and go. We welcome such daily sixty-second
refreshment on subway platforms whenever we find it, between
trains, between stations, while waiting to move on.

For example, on my way home from the office, I've stopped to
listen to a black woman who sings on the N/R line, only on
Thursdays. Then there's the Mexican orchestra leader from Paris
who plays classical violin under the stairs from time to time,
whenever he's out of a job.

But this particular sign struck a new note. And so gigantic!
"Conduct your blooming . . . " We who are glued to the city by
our jobs and our lives, where else could we bloom? No one will
disagree that the New York subway system has plenty of noise
and whip to it, and sometimes life picks us up and throws us
around like a whirlwind. No flower garden here! Yet, to para-

phrase the jewish sage, Hillel the Elder, "If not now, when? If not here, where?"

That's exactly what's so hard to take in. We are where we are, those of us who have no means to change where we live, no summer house or beach cabin. But here where we are we can either flower or fade, we can choose to vibrate with love or with self-pity.

The gods offer us this possibility: To live positively, to love passionately, within the limitations of our circumstances, within the compass of the life we have been given.

What's most important to realize this week is that we don't have to be passive about our situation. Whether the outer one is a garden or a slum dwelling, we can select our inner landscape. We can, in fact, choose (or refuse) to give up the myriad complaints and negative reactions that stir in us by recognizing them for what they are — dissatisfaction with my life. What could I change? Something is up to me. Remember that while such mutterings may seem roundly justified by your circumstances, they are useless, even though they can fill your inner life to bursting until you explode. Or implode.

Day 1
When you have time today, write down a careful description of the place you live, your difficulties, family, job. What are your feelings about them all? We always have two choices, positive or negative, affirmation or complaint. Dr. Albert Schweitzer, who received The Nobel Peace Prize in 1952, often said, "It's better to create than to protest." What can you create today?

Day 2
As you move into your day, notice how you react to the world around you. Your criticisms, your complaints, your approval ratings for every-thing you see. Write them down. Then take stock of your inner landscape. Do you feel stuck? If so, where? And where are you blessed? Now line up your protests and complaints on one side of the page and write those blessings down on the other side. "Fine," you may say. "But sometimes it feels good to get all that reaction and disappointment and

resentment out. To kvetch about it." I agree. But what I suggest is that you write it all down in your notebook rather than downloading it on your family and friends. Then, tonight, when it's in front of you in black and white, look at it carefully. Weigh both sides.

Day 3

Hopefully you'll begin to realize that a lot of what seemed rather black contains other colors. Explore that thought today. "What colors play through my life?" Take time to notice and to experiment. For example, perhaps your boss is a tyrant who makes your life miserable. I had one of those, too. She kept me on my toes as I learned to work around her, gradually freeing myself from her prison of demandingess. Easy? Never! Interesting? Yes. Even educational.

Day 4

Notice your irritation about the way things are, how you dream of another life, how you hate to be interrupted. I often sigh with impatience when one of my children calls up with a problem ("How long, O Lord, how long?"). Yet what would I do without them? If you think about it, you'll realize that while the interruption may be irritating, the inter-rupter is a gift of love. That's also true when my cat Gatsby gently scratches at my leg where I sit absorbed in writing at the computer. "How about a roll on the floor," he asks. What a good idea!

Day 5

What complaint could you sacrifice today in the fire of your wish for change? As Gurdjieff suggested, it's a big thing to sacrifice the suffering that seems inevitable as we confront the limitations of our lives and ourselves. But if we could, we might be able to live more richly and fully the life that is bequeathed to us. "Conduct your blooming" then becomes a conscious choice. That would be a flowering indeed.

Emptying the Cup

Remember the Zen story of the Buddhist scholar eager to learn from a famous Master? He rushes in, breathless, to sit at the wise man's feet, and the Master offers him some tea, pouring it into the cup until it overflows. The new disciple probably wonders if the old man is a bit gaga. In any case, he politely points out that the cup is already full. The Master replies, "You come to ask for teaching, but before I can teach you, you'll have to empty your cup."

What is our cup full of? A good guess would be reactions, complaints, longings, and lots of information, both useful and unnecessary. So what happens when we try, like the Buddhist scholar, to make contact with a deeper level of our being? We sit down, determined to find *nirvana, satori,* yesterday's successful meditation. tomorrow's ardent desire, or whatever is our idea of the perfect place to refresh ourselves inside. But to open to the infinite we need to make more space in ourselves right where we are, not go somewhere else to an ideal place.

So how can we empty our cup? Our most powerful instrument is attention. Whether we focus it on listening to our inner voices, on observing the sensations in our body, or on our breathing, we are harnessing heavy-duty help — a workhorse, so to speak. More powerful than any of us can imagine, attention is the force that creates miracles in the everyday world.

But first it must be gathered, and unfortunately our attention is spread out everywhere, all over our world. The power that could serve our aims and intentions is attracted by any and everything we see or hear or think or feel. Our attention wanders everywhere even as we maintain the illusion that we are in control of it.

How could we have lost this central power? Was it ever ours? Simone Weil insists that the whole purpose of children's education should be to teach them how to gather their attention and put it to good use. Gurdjieff says our grandmothers forgot to teach us about it. However, we can start right now, learning to gather our attention and focus it in many ways, some of them described in this book. And the task is simple (though not easy) because, as Gurdjieff also says, "you *are* where your attention is." There's a clue! We can try to be right here where we are!

Sometimes you may feel very far from home base, lost in the desert without an oasis in view, or slogging through an endless jungle of demands on your time and energy. At those times it's important to remember that there is help. There is always help. Marion Woodman suggests that you imagine you are cutting through the jungle with a machete, trudging along day after day, trying to find your way out. At last you see an open space ahead and perk up as you come to the edge of a huge river. Yay! You rejoice for a moment, thinking you've arrived at last. But as you look across the water and see there's only more jungle on the other side, you droop, discouraged. But wait a minute! As you lift your head to look again, you see to your amazement that someone else has been cutting a path through that farther jungle towards you. We are always met. We are never alone.

Day 1
The central issue may be that we are always too busy. With never time enough to be still, to be silent, our life is like the Buddhist scholar's cup, always running over. See if you can empty your cup a little today. Try to leave room for an unexpected connection with yourself. Take a few deep breaths by the window. Walk down the hall counting your steps consciously.

Day 2
Whenever you seek that place of R & R from the world's demands, do you think of it as going somewhere, as moving away from wherever you are? Try another approach today. Think of it as staying right where you are and making more space in yourself. To do this, come to a complete stop a few times in the middle of your day. First recognize how full you are of whatever's going on at that moment, worries, duties, reactions, longings. Then listen carefully to all the conflicting voices in yourself for a few minutes. How do you feel? Assess your body's needs. Get up

and stretch your arms high above your head. Remind yourself of your heart's desire.

Day 3
To test the premise that it is hard for you to keep your attention anywhere for long, try P. D. Ouspensky's exercise a few times today. Take out your watch and focus all your attention on the second hand. Each time you try this, write down how many seconds you can keep all your attention on it. You may discover that with practice you can learn to extend the time. In other words, we can train our attention if we take the time and trouble.

Day 4
When you stop to take a break, have a cup of coffee or tea, you move away from the duties and pursuits that have captured your attention. As you go through your day, begin to connect these moments consciously to your wish to be present to your life. You are creating an invisible necklace of momentary gems. Then, each time you go back to work, remind yourself of F. M. Alexander's admonition: "We must cultivate . . . the deliberate habit of taking up every occupation with the whole mind, with a living desire to carry each action through to a successful accomplishment, a desire which necessitates bringing into play every faculty of the attention."

Day 5
Each time you turn away from your busyness, take a momentary impression of yourself with all three of your perceiving organs at the same time — mind, body and feeling. Gurdjieff calls this "taking snapshots." As your thought reminds you to take the photo, notice the state of your body and feelings instantly and honestly. What's going on with all three of these functions at this very moment? Write it down. Begin to collect snapshots for a future album.

Wrong Again?

Some people are either sure they are right or convinced they're always wrong. I was told as a child that I was "often wrong but never doubtful." Years later, I realized that hidden behind my pseudo-confidence was a self-accuser, convinced that once again she'd messed up. It wasn't till midlife that Rumi shot an arrow of hope straight into my heart, offering an escape from both extremes: "Out beyond ideas of wrong-doing and right doing, there is a field," he said. "I'll meet you there."

We all need to find that field. What a tremendous relief it can be to know that beyond guilt and responsibility, beyond sin and redemption, there is a place of rest. Rest for my busy mind, always arguing, elaborating, affirming, condemning, criticizing. Rest for my anguished heart, seeking meaning in a confused world full of conflicting demands. And rest from the insidious fear that "I'll be caught out because, in spite of my good intentions, I'll get it wrong again."

"Does this field exist in time or is it timeless?" I wonder. Surely I need to find time to go there, to turn away from my busy life and listen to the spaces between the many words I say and hear. Or even attend to the sound of silence itself. Yet sometimes this space between my doings and achievings emerges all by itself, in the midst of "business as usual." The ordinary pressures, obligations, and efforts to get things done fall away, and suddenly I'm alone and free of anxiety in a non-invasive space that doesn't demand action but provides nourishment. I call this space Endless Time. In it I feel cared for, reassured by a non-demanding relationship with life, liberated from the sense that I must perform, get stuff done, realize a potential, serve a cause, help a friend.

The fact is, Endless Time has always been there, though I seldom realize it. It waits for me, ready to flood in whenever I have sense enough to stop and lay down my perceived burdens. If I can give up for a moment the problems that seem so important, so imme-diate, so real, then I will find myself immersed in another order of reality — the world of touch, taste, smell, and unrecognized feelings that accompany me at this very moment.

You might think Endless Time is like prayer or meditation, as in casting off the cares of the day for a private moment of quiet in the back room. But the funny thing is that this wider space can open just as easily on a crowded subway platform where a home-bound mass of humanity hurries to their next thing. Unexpectedly I exchange a look with a fellow passenger or somehow feel connected to these rushing lives, as full of joy and fear and investments in relationships as mine. Then the noise recedes and inner quiet floods in from a world beyond time.

Rumi's field beyond wrong-doing and right doing is waiting for all of us. But it's a choice we make. If you choose to go there, attend again and yet again to what is going on in you and in the world, without judgment or condemnation. Even sometimes allow a love for the fractured and suffering humanity around and in you to enter your busy field of action. You function between heaven and earth, between extremes, and you are usually more than adequate to the task of living.

Day 1
Today you are hoping to find a door into that field. Whenever you have a moment of spontaneous release today, write down what you were thinking or doing just then. Try to discover what interrupted the usual concerns and invite it to visit you again. Begin to link such moments in your mind as if you were putting together a necklace. Set the most recent gem in your heart like a jewel you can cherish through your day. Wear it in good health.

Day 2
See if you can value those moments consciously, rather than let them slip by uncelebrated. Perhaps you can learn to extend such unexpected fragments of freedom from deadlines and stress. For example, when such a moment offers itself today, "take five," as in five deep breaths. Or why not take time for a cup of coffee then and there, as you listen to the many sounds of the world and the many voices in yourself.

Day 3

Begin to notice what is beautiful anywhere you go. Timeless moments often appear when we are face to face with beauty. For example, when I'm in the park, my eyes rise with the powerful branches of trees as they reach up to the sky, and I feel a surge of joy rise with them. Or maybe I'm walking home from the office, lost in thought, eyes on the ground, until I spy a tiny green shoot struggling up between two slabs of concrete on the pavement. My heart goes out to that tiny life, hoping to affirm itself in a demanding world, just like you and me.

Day 4

One barrier to opening ourselves to inner quiet is fear. A flower at the peak of its perfection is unafraid that it will be gone tomorrow. But we aren't like that! We know nothing lasts. Yet consider a timeless moment you have had, perhaps by the sea, when your busy thoughts are suddenly hushed by the silence between one wave and another. It's a moment you'll have with you always, if you choose to turn to it again. In the same way, try today to listen to the silence between the sounds of life, or between the words you speak, or between the thoughts in your mind.

Day 5

To deepen such timeless moments, you must cherish them. Invent reminders that require you to pay attention to what's delicate and beautiful. Take something fragile with you to work — a shell, pebble, petal, beautiful museum postcard — anything that might call you back to Rumi's field. I often place a flower in the middle of my desk at the office, in constant danger of being crushed by my busyness. Only my active remembering will keep it safe.

Nowhere to Go

Is it so terrible, the thought that I'm not 'getting' anywhere? I used to concentrate on the hurdles in my path as if each day were a straight line into the future, over barriers. But the problem with 'getting ahead' is that it is two-dimensional — I move into an imaginary future that may have nothing to do with reality. And what's worse, in my concentration on the goal ahead, I lose contact with what's above and below.

Above lies the possibility of connecting with a larger level of mind and feeling. Below is the sensible and sensate planting of my feet on the earth of reality. Yet again and again I choose to see my life as if it were an arrow shooting straight forward to a target. If I can release the mind's hold on that approach, I am offered the possibility of living in the immediate moment. All my energy of thought and feeling — formerly focused on getting ahead, accomplishing feats of derring-do, or just plain getting through the day — shifts into a completely different reality. That of me, here, now.

Not that it's easy — daunting to say the least — to let go of the projection of my life and its meaning into the future, whether ten years from now or this very afternoon. So much hope is geared to "someday" when I'll find what I long for. My handsome prince may be just around the corner or the CEO's three-window office might soon be mine. To give all that up is to face the unknown, to let go of the future and remain in the living present, the only reality of my life.

Thankfully, there's always help if I ask for it, and the help is right here and now, where I stand. Although I tend to undervalue the body and its experiences, without a physical sensation of myself, where will the energy that could fill me find a place to land? As soon as my thought is turned toward the sensation of myself, I become free of the prison of past memories and future longings. New feelings begin to appear, as if attracted by a magnet.

I am here. I am present. What does that mean? My head's not wandering or turning in circles around a few repetitive thoughts. I'm aware of my body and its joys and complaints. As the body feels accepted, appreciated, given its due, an inner door opens to a new sense of presence, a lack of fear, an attentive listening and watching, not moving faster than I am able to follow myself in movement.

Nourished by this state, affirmed in body, mind and feeling, I experience all three elements:

Me.
Here.
Now.

Me is the being. Here and now depend on the quality of my attention, and whether mind and body accept to live the present moment together, without fear or avoidance.

Let's say you accept what I'm saying as an idea, even as a wish. You truly wish to be present, but suspect that when you turn your attention to what's going on in your body/being, you'll discover that you are achy or just plain tired. That's no fun! Nevertheless, while it's uncomfortable to feel tired, you need to learn to bear the experiences of your shifting states of energy, because that's what's really happening. To stay open to the present, you must firmly commit to finding out what's really going on right now.

Day 1
The present moment is an interrogatory state. The minute you ask, "What's going on?" or "What am I up to?" you are right here. But in the next moment your mind will probably comment on what you've discovered. Or your attention will be attracted by something "out there." Your relationship with the present has disappeared. So, for today, experiment with those two questions. Ask them often, and write down whatever the answer might be. Then ask again a little while later.

Day 2
To live in the present is to live in the unknown, which can sometimes be pretty uncomfortable. Most of us like to be in charge, in control, so we tend to eliminate as many unknowns as possible. But, for today, exper-

iment with how much you can accept, at any given moment, of what's unknown to you. Look around and inside yourself from time to time, and tally up what you don't know about what's going on. It's not just a thought inquiry. Turn to your body as well. How does it feel? What didn't you know about it a moment before you asked? As Kakuzo Okakura says in The Book of Tea, *"The art of life lies in a constant readjustment to our surroundings." To readjust, you need to be fully present.*

Day 3
The call to live in the present doesn't mean you shouldn't plan for tomorrow. The future is a result of the preparation and training and learning that take place in the present tense. So here-and-now is where your attention needs to be poised, as you lay the groundwork for being present in your tomorrows. Try this today: set an alarm in your watch or remind yourself to wake up to your present Self every two hours and, at that moment, ask yourself what you are doing to prepare your future.

Day 4
Whatever you plan or hope for in the future, you will be helped by living more deeply, more consciously, more sensitively in this life that's already yours. Like the thousand mile journey that begins with the first step, each new moment offers you another chance to begin. So today ask yourself, "What makes something new? Where does new come from?" Also notice the feeling or sensation of "old." Children know more about new than we do because so much is new to them. And they bring a fresh instrument to the task. Can you follow Jesus' suggestion, to "become as a little child"? Adopt a child's-eye view today, as you try to look freshly at what's in front of you.

Day 5
Here's another exercise that might help. Just as each day begins with new energy, each breath also represents a cycle. It's brief and it's in the present, right here and now. You can breathe in the new at any moment. And as you breathe out, let go of any old complaints and annoyances, that nagging sense of failure, or whatever judgmental attitudes hold you back from a life of inner freedom. Breathe out the Old; breathe in the New!

Ariadne's Thread

As a child I loved the story of Ariadne, imagining myself as the innocent, beautiful young princess who fell in love with a handsome prince, long ago in far-off Crete. Destined to walk the Labyrinth, to meet and be meat for the Minotaur, Theseus was a sacrifice to the powerful male god-monster.

But love attracts love and, like all of us (whether we know it or not), Ariadne had a fairy godmother who gave her a golden thread with which to save him. He was told to attach it to a stone at the entrance before he went in so that no matter how complex the turnings of the Labyrinth might be, he could find his way out.

My attention is like that golden thread. It designates a way out of driving ambition, lackadaisical boredom, or any state in which I'm lost to myself-as-I-am. I try to tug at it often in the middle of the daily labyrinth of my life, but I can never hold onto it for long. Again and again I lose it, even when I take it up purposefully.

Here I am, hoping to stay in touch with myself and my wish to be present, while my body sits, walks or does stuff in real time. But when I'm tangled up in the confusions of my life, I forget. My attention disappears from me-here-now to invest itself in something out there, until I feel again the tug of the thread, the need to be connected to myself. What can remind me to attempt the return to home base? Why is it so hard to remember that I carry a secret thread in my soul's hand wherever I go, which could help me return to the sense of myself here and now? I guess the remembering is just as important as the thread itself.

I've lost that thread of attention a thousand, thousand times. I do something or go somewhere, firmly determined to keep it in my grasp. And just as many times I wake up to discover I've already dropped it. "What could help me maintain the thread of my attention?" I ask myself. "Look for an anchor," replies my inner guide.

So I try to anchor my attention on my body — my butt on the chair, my feet on the ground, my fingers tapping at the computer, my hand clutching the pen or the cup.

Finally I begin to accept that I'm always going to lose it. Lucky for me it doesn't lose me! It's always there, waiting to be picked up again, ready to guide me once more toward a deeper relationship with my Self.

Your attention is a powerful instrument that can lead you back to yourself. (Wise Theseus knew he'd better concentrate. For him it was a matter of life or death!) But do you value it enough? We tend to let our attention wander anywhere, following a thought, a colorful dress or a face in the crowd. We don't understand how precious this faculty is, or how little control we have over it. Yet in order to become more aware of ourselves, and the world around us, in a full-bodied, caring way, we need to be able to keep and focus our attention. This week try to discover how important your attention really is, and how little control you have over it. Think of holding onto that thread as if it were a life or death issue, as Theseus did.

Day 1
From time to time today, look at the second hand of your watch as you try to remain aware of yourself. Focus all your attention on your body/mind and the movement of the second hand. Don't allow passing thoughts to interrupt your concentration. How long can you remain present? For many people, the mind wanders off in search of something "more interesting" in less than a minute.

Day 2
As you walk down a busy street or mall today, decide that for two minutes (or one block) you'll refuse to let your attention be distracted by other people or colorful store windows. Keep your attention on your body/mind as you move. Then, for the next two minutes or the next block, allow yourself to look at everything that attracts you, noticing how your attention is pulled in every direction. Alternate these two experiences several times as you walk along. How hard is it to stay focused on yourself walking? How easy to let the attention flow out toward whatever distracts you?

Day 3

Today, hold your attention more consciously on the actual work you are doing, whether at a computer, making dinner, or anything else. Stay with what your hands are doing. Concentrate your mind on them. You can also experiment with attending to your feet on the ground. Wherever you are standing or walking there is a continual connection to the earth, our mother. Tune into it. Sense the pull of gravity.

Day 4

Try the following exercise to help keep your attention on yourself: As you walk along the street or mall or country road or even down the hall to your bosses office, notice the sensation on the bottom of your feet as you press the floor with each step you take. When you've done that a few times, begin to count your steps in rhythm: 1, 2, 3, 4 — 4, 3, 2, 1. Proceed to 2, 3, 4, 5, etc. and once you get to 12, 11, 10, 9, start counting backward in the same way. You may find it both demanding and irritating to maintain your count and focus on your feet at the same time, but after a few minutes you'll probably feel more alive, more present. You'll discover a new relationship between the equipment with which you think and the body in which you live.

Day 5

The rest of the week, try to see how your attention is taken, whether you like it or not, by everything from wandering thoughts to outer distractions. Invent your own exercises to stay alert and aware of mind and body as you sit or move. Write them down for possible future use. And at any moment, as you move around in your day, reach for your own golden thread. It's always there, waiting for you.

Finding the Right Place

The Shaker hymn sings about "The Place That Is Right" but how do you get there? Often it's just about impossible. Sometimes it seems to depend on the moon, the tides, the inner weather — the waxing and waning of emotional reactions. Who knows when the pull of Ariadne's golden thread might lead unexpectedly to a place that is right?

Hard to find or not, everyone needs such a place, both inside and outside themselves, where they can find rest, contentment or solace. My own Right Place would be somewhere quiet, perhaps a meadow high on a hill where I can smell the grass, hear the buzz of insects, and feel the heartbeat of the earth pulsing beneath me. I would think and not think at the same time, for thoughts would come and go like the clouds passing overhead.

Where is that right place for you? A wide beach where you can lie and listen to the shushing of the waves? Or deep in the woods, where you can almost touch the light as it slants through the leaves? A mountaintop where you are literally on top of the world? Water, woods, and mountains help tune us in to another pace, a slower rhythm of life.

But if you are unable to travel, find the nearest tree. Trees are the guardians of the natural world and invite you into that natural rhythm. If you stand still long enough in front of a tree, imagining its roots growing toward you underground while the branches soar overhead protectively, its strength will reach out to support you. Listen! You can almost hear the tree grow!

Wherever your secret place may be, there's a path to it if you are willing to pay the price. But to find it you need to slow down, and who is willing to do that? Nevertheless, it is a good way to connect with this inner/outer natural world, whether in meadow, beach, woodland, or wherever you are standing or sitting right now.

If you slow down and turn inward, everything that's moving around inside you will simmer down, just as if you turned the heat down on a boiling stew. You don't have to wait for vacation or exhaustion to lead you to another, more restful mode. Just slow down as you intentionally connect with the world of Being, with your Self.

You'd probably love to zip off to beach, woods or mountain spa, but that may not be in the cards or in your wallet. So let's see how you might find a centering place without the support of such beautiful natural surroundings, in what we sometimes refer to as the Real World. There you sit at home or in your office, at a meeting, a concert, a school performance by one of your kids, or even in church; bored, or perhaps too tired to listen. Oh dear! What to do so as not to fall asleep in front of everyone? How to crank yourself awake to get the assignment done, listen intelligently, or avoid embarrassing your family by snoring at the show. Wouldn't it be great to feel more alive, more yourself, right in the middle of this place where you may not want to be! At least once each day this week try the following exercise.

Step 1
First, scoot your butt to the back of your chair as you straighten up, allowing your back to rest upright against it. Then find your sit-bones at the base of the torso (you can sit on your hands for a moment to find these two bony protuberances) and visualize how the spine rises up from them. Let your whole torso become a strong column, like the trunk of a tree.

Step 2
Next, imagine your spine is Jacob's ladder rising to heaven, and you a small person who can clamber up the rungs on tiny feet, all the way from the sacrum, vertebra by vertebra (24 of them), to the tippy-top, where the skull sits on your spine. The highest vertebra is higher than you might think, located right up inside the skull, behind your eyes and between your ears. It's called the Atlas, and that's where we carry the world on our shoulders. So climb all the way up, rung by rung, and at the top invite the head to float up off the spine.

Step 3

Once you have found your way up there in your mind's eye, stay there and, at the same time, begin to think of the opposite direction: down. It's always useful to think in two directions at once — your head surging up off your spine while your sit-bones sink deep into the chair, where the earth supports your weight so you don't have to. The spine is made happy by that thought, and as it lengthens you can relax.

Step 4

Now close your eyes and ask yourself, "What's under the chair?" Try to see it in your mind's eye, without sneaking a look. Maybe a candy wrapper, perhaps your briefcase, umbrella, or the bag of stuff you bought on the way there. Next, move your awareness from under the seat to whatever you think is on your left side, still with eyes closed. Maybe it's another chair on which a person you like, or don't like, is sitting. Focus your mind's eye on them. What are they wearing? Then, after a moment, shift your query to the space on your right as you ask the same questions. Next, after at least a minute, turn your attention to what's above your head. What color is the ceiling? Then, what's behind your chair and at the back of the room?

Step 5

Finally, turn your focus on what you imagine is in front of you. That's where we live most of the time. It usually takes up all our attention. As you open your eyes, focus your attention on your own body/being. Here you are! Look all around to see what you remembered and what you missed. Then ask yourself, "Am I still sleepy, bored, and uncomfortable?" Silently try to describe to yourself how you feel right now. What words apply?

Two Worlds —
One Human Being

The relationship between the head and the body is a continuing enigma — they so often seem disconnected from each other. For one thing, they don't speak the same language. And just like the heart, the body has its reasons that reason cannot understand.

When I'm present to my body, I often feel serene. Unless I'm in pain or in a panic, there's a living-in-the-moment contentment that streams in through the senses. It's good to be alive. Simple pleasures delight me; or just sitting here, bathed in awareness. But sooner or later I begin to wonder: "Am I too passive, too mindless? Me-here-now is fine, but what about the intellect-in-action?"

So I turn to the world of the head brain where I can also feel good. When I'm thinking my way through my life, I'm in charge. My intellectual machinery is put to good use to reason through a problem, gather data for an article, or study up on neuroscience. The downside is an aching back from working too long at the computer, or reading curled up in a chair.

The head brain's work-ethic attitude presses me onward, exhorting me to get busy with something "worthwhile." But why? Surely my mind should serve as a kind of informational calculator that simply tells me: this is black; that is white. This road will take you here; that one to another place. While the body, on the other hand, is experiential — alive to what's going on in and around me at this very moment. My psycho-physical presence, embodied here for a little while, is lit by another light.

So here I sit, trying to coordinate two aspects of myself, two opposing voices that occupy a single organism. From one side I'm told to relax and enjoy the moment, listen to the world, notice the blooming flowers, while the other interrupts with, "There's lots to do and too little time to do it in. Don't waste time sitting around. Only by being active can you improve yourself, approve of yourself, solve your problems, maintain your job, care for your parents, support your children."

"Hey, wait a minute!" I implore. "What supports *me*?" Because this present contentment nourishes me, even as my 'doing' mechanism urges me on to greater efforts. Are these twp sides of me always at war? Is there a bridge that connects them? Can both participate in my life at the same moment? Or am I always wasting time when I'm not doing something? In anguish, I cry "Which is better?" As the tension becomes unbearable, an authoritative inner voice addresses the issue: "What could be better than being yourself?" There it is. I am two, with a lifetime assignment to become one conscious human being.

It's not pleasant to accept that you are divided, and sometimes hard to figure out who should be in charge at any given moment. And, unfortunately, your head can't make the final judgment call. It is great for evaluating and separating white from black. It can apply reason to what's going on, but it will always be unable to embrace the central issue of **you,** *because it is only part of the reality of your life. This week ask your big questions of the whole of yourself, engaging heart, body, and mind simultaneously.*

Day 1

For today, make an effort to learn the language of the body. It always lives in the present tense. That means it will have an immediate response any time you tune into its preferences. Engage with it from time to time as you go through the day. Ask, "What do I want right now? How do I feel? Where do I ache? Am I hungry? Do I need a rest or a cup of coffee or to get out of this chair and go for a walk?" Or any question you think appropriate to the moment you are in. Then listen — really listen. There will always be an answer though it may sometimes seem like Greek to you.

Day 2

Today the operative question is, "Who's in charge?" If you have a watch with an alarm, set it for every two hours. When it goes off, ask yourself,

"Who's running my show right now?" The only hope you have — or anyone has — of choosing wisely where to engage your energy, is to see what's really going on. Once you know that, you have a choice. Otherwise, as we charge along through our day, unquestioning, what choice is there?

Day 3
Any effort to stay in the present moment may give rise to a hidden fear of bad news: Will I discover that I'm imperfect, inadequate, ordinary and unsatisfactory? When I make such judgments, I'm pushed away from the present moment, determined to improve, to move forward. But that may be an escape from seeing what is. If such a fear holds you back, challenge yourself today. Ask yourself, as I did, "What is really better" What at this or any given moment are the rules I am living by, judging by?"

Day 4
Perhaps today you can cut a few of the ties that bind you to the one who thinks he or she is running the show. That would allow you to float free and see what's really going on, separated from the opinions and judgments of one aspect of yourself or another. However, you may find, as I often do, that a powerful current keeps you running and driving yourself onward to some future goal. Remind yourself that however good it is to have an aim, it's not so good to be driven, or to occupy a fixed position, or to be caught in someone else's flow. If that current is always driving you away from the present moment, can you dare to spend a few minutes right here, right now?

Day 5
Now that you have a sense of the current that pulls you away, begin to wonder whether there may not be an undercurrent that pulls you toward your Self. After all, why are you reading this book? You have a real wish to come home to your Self. Think of it as a still small voice that can sometimes become a whirlwind or, if it helps, call it the voice of God. When all else fails, imagine yourself in a rowboat floating merrily downstream in the current of everyday life. Then turn your boat around and face upstream. You may not be able to paddle against the strong current until the water is quieter. But you are alive to the power of the river and you are turned towards home.

Making a New Start

Oh, how I long, you long, we all long to begin all over again. But making a new start isn't about starting again. There's no again about it — new is new. Once you realize how quickly you can slip back into the old ways, you'll agree that making a new start needs constant renewing. That means you have to work at the "new" part at the same time that everything is calling you back to the old. As F. M. Alexander said, "Change involves carrying out an activity against the habit of life."

Hard put to find words to describe this active work of renewal, I'll try to recount my own experience with it. First, there's a moment of truth: I've connected with my life on a deeper level than before. With a vision of a new understanding I can base my life on, I'm determined to change for the better. However, very soon old habits of thought and feeling come flooding back in and my clarity of purpose fades away like a receding tide. How to withstand the pull of that undertow? I used to think direct combat was a viable solution but have been swept away many a time. You can't do battle head-on with a big wave. Instead, you must learn to dive through it.

Take New Year's Day, for example. Our ordinary work life comes to a halt as holiday fever takes over, followed by the madness, joy and sadness repeated each year at this time: Christmas, Hanukah and shopping; caroling and wrapping presents; concerts, parties, cooking and stuffing ourselves with goodies. But all of it comes to an end on January first, as we face those devout wishes, solemn vows, and "irreversible" decisions sworn in the heat of our desire to change. However light or solemn these vows may be, now the dues must be paid — the price of admission to a new life.

A new beginning needs food. You have to nourish it each day. My head makes lists with MEDITATION and WALKS IN THE PARK in capital letters. But if my determination is not to be a hollow pretence, I need to be able to awaken to that new vision right in the middle of the action. What's certain is that my old whip-cracking approach to my new vows will be as ineffectual as it has always been, once the first few days of forcing myself to comply have passed.

That means this new vision has to develop some muscle to become a reality. In other words, I need to remember my wish for the new life when it really counts, when my good intentions tend to unravel. The challenge of keeping our new resolutions comes down to this: how to remember the new direction in the middle of the old habit?

Never think this tentative wish for a new beginning is a small thing. It's very big. However, it often seems more like an intuition. Our inner ear isn't open to that still, small voice amid the hustle of our lives, the hubbub of the marketplace, or the urgent pressure from within ourselves to do all that we feel we OUGHT to do.

Day 1
Your first assignment is to stop. Before beginning a new project or a new day, take time to listen to your inner voices. Believe it or not, we have to learn to listen. Otherwise, the flow of our thoughts and desires just takes us along automatically downstream, like the flow of life.

Day 2
How to discover what you really value? That's a work in itself. Sift through your life of pressures and quick-relief solutions to your heart's desire. Find a real wish. And, to begin with, any real wish will do. Write down on a piece of paper the first real wish that surges up. Maybe you've always secretly longed to paint or sing or write a book, or you wanted to be alone more often or take a walk in the park every day. Take time to think about it often today.

Day 3
Any of a thousand hidden wishes in your wishing well is a great start. Once it's discovered and articulated, separate a little more time for that wish every day. Not only will it free you from the prison of your habitual thinking and doing, it can also lead you to a more authentic life. When

you honor your hidden wishes by giving time to them, you enter into a new relationship with your Self. You needn't push to perform because your new practice begins to lead you in the direction of your heart's desire. Allow time for it today.

Day 4

Study your everyday habits, both physical and emotional. At any moment you can tune in to habitual attitudes or automatic states of tension, and ask, "What's going on?" If you want to allow this inner call to grow louder, you will have to take some form of action. For example, if you wish to stay alert to what's going on, to be more awake in your life, there are a number of things you could try. Experiment with setting an alarm clock every so often, or doing counting exercises or writing in a journal. Remind yourself that tomorrow may never come. A moment of calm reflection, or even a slowing down of your pace, could transform your state in a moment, for a moment. Which will you try right now?

Day 5

Here's an exercise I call "planting seeds of change." Try it today. Every time you wake up to the Old, find some way to plant a seed of New against the force of habit. Let's say my old nemesis, Mrs. Rigid, appears, clutching her rulebook and telling me just how things ought to be done. I take a step back before she has a chance to swallow me up, reminding myself how terrified she is of change — that's what makes her rigid. But I don't have to be stuck in her narrow-minded world, or follow the same laws she does. A seed has been planted. When you notice your demand-ingness — the Autocrat in action — take a step back, an inner withdrawal from the belief that he's right. Don't try to shoot him down. He's too powerful for that! But separate yourself. Ask what he wants. Do you want what he wants? Perhaps not. Another seed. When will your new seeds sprout? How big will the fruit or flower be? No idea. Perhaps it's not for us to know at our level of engagement. But decide to trust that planting new seeds into the old way of doing things will be a meaningful 'yes' to your deep wish to live differently.

Where Am I?

Whenever we amaze or horrify ourselves, when we wake up to the sudden conviction that there's more to our lives than the surface discloses, we may utter the anguished Socratic cry, "Who am I?" It can bring a sense of relief as it awakens a resonance in us, widening our inner horizon, adding depth to the most inconsequential moment. To ask it is to begin to follow a path.

But there's another question at the heart of my search for personal authenticity. While "Who am I?" evokes an unknown, which may forever be so, "Where am I?" creates a place from which to begin. It's a surefire wake-up call to attend to my presence here and now. Where am I in my inner and outer world? What's my body doing? Where's my thought drifting? What am I reacting to?

For centuries seekers of presence have turned to yoga and dance for a daily practical reminder of spirit. The repetitive rituals used by Jews and Sufis in prayer also serve as a kinesthetic experience that tells them where they are in space. And the Shakers long ago discovered how dance could center them in worship. In not-so-spiritual circles, runners seek their "high" and athletes strive for the "zone" of maximum performance, echoing the possibility open to all of us of finding momentary balance at the center of our psycho-physical world.

It is here on earth, in this body/mind, that the perhaps eternal being that I am functions, even if I am mostly unaware of it. So if at any given moment I ask myself: "Where am I?" I'll find a sense of myself located somewhere in my body and in space. When I made this experiment just now, I discovered that "me" seemed to be located somewhere in my upper body, between my chest and my throat. It was about a foot high and paper-thin, and it had no back at all. How could I have been so unaware of the life coursing through this complex coordination that I am? As I awakened to other parts of my body, I also became aware of the state of my energy, which revved up. Surprise! The body likes me to take it into account!

Whenever I invite the question "Where am I?" to resonate through me, my kinesthetic awareness expands to include my whole physical presence — and much more. To ask, "Where am I?" connects mind and body in the practice of my own presence. As I search for an answer, I'm invited to participate in a renewed experience of myself. At such moments I reaffirm my existence on this planet — flesh, blood, bones and brains, all waking up to the possibility of being right here, right now.

Each time you ask yourself this magical question, be quick to notice just what you actually perceive of yourself. Is your immediate sensation of yourself confined to a small part of your body-being, perhaps only to your head or chest? Begin each day by opening gradually to the experience of yourself from top to toe, allowing yourself to fully occupy your own space as you acquire more width and depth. You are three-dimensional, although you may sometimes feel two-dimensional, like a cardboard cutout doll.

Day 1
At any time you ask the question "Where am I?", give that first impression of a limited "you" some kind of measurement: is it two feet high and very thin? Three feet square? I've done this many times, often shocked to discover how small is the sense of where I am located in myself. And it's not always in the same place, but most often around the head and chest. How about you? Try it several times today.

Day 2
As you go through the day today, pay attention to your arms and hands as they busy themselves with whatever work needs to be done. Ask yourself, as often as you remember, what your right hand is up to. And look for moments when you can sense how the two hands work together in concert, truly related to each other. Our hands sometimes know how to do things better when our heads stop bossing them around. D. T. Suzuki, author of many books on Zen, said, "a man learns to think with his hands." What does that mean to you?

Day 3

Any time you've been sitting for a while, ask yourself, "Where are my legs?" Were you in fact aware of them at all? Legs scarcely exist in our consciousness when we're sitting, especially when we work at a computer or play games on a handheld device. At such times we are totally engaged in the screen in front of us. Sure, when you stand up your legs have no choice but to go into active mode to support you, and that's a whole other experience, but what part do they play in your attempt to be present when you are sitting down? Make an effort to include them in your awareness today, even when they aren't active.

Day 4

Today, as you move around doing whatever you do. focus on the fact that there's a head floating at the top of your spine. Think of your head riding on top of you like a howdah bobbing on an elephant's back. Each time you relax the neck muscles that tend to grip the skull, the Atlanto-occipital joint releases, giving a friendly wakeup tug on the spine. The release of this major connecting joint between the skull and the top of the spine invites all of the other joints in your body to release any unnecessary holding on.

Day 5

Today is Torso day. Seek to become aware of the fact that you take it wherever you go. A lot happens in the torso that you are mostly unconscious of. It's where your heart beats, for one thing, as your kidneys excrete and your liver processes, not to mention the other parts of a very busy digestive system. Most important, the torso is home to breathing. It is a mighty storage tank of energy that has permitted you to survive till now and will last the rest of your life. As you expand your awareness to a richer, fuller impression of yourself, ask yourself often, "Where am I now?" And again, "now?"

Wait Like a Hunter

Do you ever wake up in the morning feeling empty — no energy to make decisions or carry out a plan you made last night? This morning I couldn't get myself going, not even to meditate or do Tai Chi. Boy, was I tired! Only after I set off to work, forcing myself into a brisk walk, did I realize my problem wasn't with the body. It was with the heart. I was empty of feeling, perhaps depressed (a life challenge like no other). Happily, once acknowledged, my state of tension and fear eased. But the emptiness remained. What to do?

In such a situation, a metaphor can be very helpful. From the Hindu point of view, Shakti, my earth energy, lives here in me, curled up asleep at the center of my Being. She is waiting for Shiva, cosmic consciousness, to seek her out. When a ray of his sun touches her, she will reach up for his embrace — just what's needed to illumine and warm the heart. But my first task is to wait for his appearance, for "I" to descend into "me."

We do a lot of waiting. Life's like that. Waiting for bus or train, for the boss to give me a raise, for my own true love to find me, for the end of something that may actually be a new beginning. We all wait in front of the Unknown, facing illness, depression or loss, or even the Next Big Step in life. Which job should I take? Which road should I travel? Where do I really want to go? And we often wait in the dark. For help; for light. Why are things the way they are? Why do terrible things happen to those I love? Why do good people do bad things? What should I do next?

Waiting can be boring or fraught with possibilities. But unless I stay alert like the six wise virgins in the Bible, I may not recognize a new possibility when it appears. Waiting for Shiva offers a new approach, inviting a tentative new openness to whatever may come.

Here's another analogy. Some time ago I heard an unhappy man complain to a wise elder. Perhaps he was empty or depressed, or simply longed to understand why, although he'd spent many years trying to get rid of the things in himself he didn't like, the change he longed for just hadn't come about. His teacher advised him to "wait like a hunter." A hunter will stand behind a tree or a rock for many hours, as still as the landscape, waiting for his prey to appear.

In order to wait like a hunter, I must learn to sit very still, to take control of my squirming or lax body/mind so it can be quiet but very alive, ready to act instantly when the time comes. Knowing myself as I do, it sounds like that could take a long time to learn! But the time won't be wasted if it's in the name of my deepest wish: to grow into the person I was born to be.

We often feel a general helplessness when we have to wait for a change in our situation or our inner state. The first step is to take stock. We are gifted with three major sending and receiving stations — head, heart and body. Whatever's holding back the flow of our energy may lie in any one or all of them.

Day 1
Start by investigating what's going on. See if you can figure out in which of these three aspects of yourself the barrier to your usual energy lies. Then begin a dialogue with yourself, and accept to listen to whatever messages appear. Embrace what you perceive as the difficulty rather than trying to squelch it in hopes of feeling better. Write down as much as you can about what seems to be going on.

Day 2
Once you suspect where the source of your difficulty lies, ask a direct question of body, mind or heart. You'll be amazed at how much your functions can tell you about what's wrong if you are open to the unknown. Don't demand answers but ask for information. Whatever the response is, it will probably come in a language you aren't used to. Each part of your personal troika speaks a different language, but each depends on the others. Practice listening to your 'other' Self.

Day 3

Sometimes it helps to come at the difficulty sideways. Offer yourself to the experiment by writing a poem to your problem. Call up a friend or take your inner questioning to a yoga class. Make some move that might help clarify or improve your understanding of what's happening inside you. Our states always carry a message. The difficulty is in how to parse it.

Day 4

As you broaden your outlook to include whichever part of you is angry, complaining or just plain suffering, acknowledge that it imprisons you in a rather small world. If you can discover a myth or analogy that applies to your situation, it will give you a larger perspective without pulling you away from what's going on. Relate your difficulty to the experiences of other human beings throughout the centuries. The Greek myths offered thousands of people a way to orient their suffering in a larger context. Fairytales represent major life challenges. What particular myth, fairytale or analogy most applies to what you are going through today?

Day 5

Finally, accept whatever is there, even if you feel empty. Be present to your state as you wait for a shift, a change in your circumstances. Everything changes sooner or later. Neither joy nor sorrow lasts, so your stuck places will come unstuck sooner or later. You can help that process by participating more consciously at every stage if you wait actively, like a hunter.

The "Should" Polarities

Life is full of shoulds. Gotta do this, gotta do that. Sometimes I wonder, is there another way to live? I tend to put the blame for my sense of duty on the need to be grown up. Adults have responsibilities, etc. However, memory tells me that my pressure to perform was just as real when I was a child. There were an awful lot of things I felt I should do. I never allowed myself much choice in the matter, so I've always pushed forward.

A few years ago I began to question why Pushing Forward was my middle name. Why was I always on the go, forever accomplishing one more thing before I let myself go to bed at night? My huge discovery: every time you push, you get pushed back. In fact, this is science — Newton's Third Law ("The mutual forces of action and reaction between two bodies are equal, opposite and collinear"). That means that for every *should* I force myself to accomplish, there is going to be an equal reaction in the opposite direction. In other words, everything I make myself do for some tyrannical inner Should God creates a powerful wave of refusal or resentment that sooner or later will catch up with me and knock me down.

Did you ever apply Newton's Third Law to yourself? What if, inside each of us, there's both a good guy who gets things done — the Achiever, the Pleaser, the Little Friend of All the World — and a rebel. Lots of people think that rebel should be quashed. I certainly did. But the rebel is telling me something really useful. And it's not so much about *what* I'm doing as about *how* I'm doing it. Sometimes I push my mind and my body too far, as if I were begging for exhaustion, illness and missed deadlines.

And if I quash the rebel for too long as I push and press to meet the *shoulds* of life, I become depressed. Many people find this, maybe you, too. We get to feeling empty, even paralyzed, unable to move forward. Note the important verb, *feeling*. Where have all our feelings gone? Where is the sense of myself as a human being? Wow! It was all sucked up into a *should!* A *should* is an enemy of the people, an enemy of feeling, an enemy of my body and an enemy of my freedom to choose.

When I question more deeply the reason behind this push-and-get-shoved-back way of living, I discover another disconcerting truth: If I'm too busy with my *shoulds*, I could be avoiding what I really ought to be doing. Like many people in this high-pressure society, I take refuge in busyness in order to avoid seeing that I've wandered too far from home territory, away from the possibility of being present to my life as it unfolds. Jungian analyst James Hollis, in *Swamplands of the Soul*, calls it self-estrangement. And he says the only way out would be to face what we are defending ourselves against with all our *shoulds*. "What task are we avoiding?" he asks. "What wants to come into the world through you?"

If you think it's time for you to follow a new path, or to discover what your task really is, first of all, you need to begin to differentiate among the many things you do. While our **shoulds** *may seem similar to each other, they are not. Each thing we think or do has a certain value, and because should-energy can kill off feeling, we easily lose a sense of the value of what we choose to undertake as we plunge ahead to accomplish it.*

Day 1
Write down what value you ascribe to the tasks you feel you must complete today, giving each task a value in importance from 1 to 10. At the end of the day, check your list of must-do assignments, the ones you truly had to push through whatever the cost. As you reevaluate them in the light of hindsight, ask yourself what price you paid for getting each of them done, in time, energy and your relationships with others, as well as your connection to your Self.

Day 2
Now begin to study these values. Does the value you put on a particular job lie in the fact that it makes money, helps others, solves problems for others or yourself, or is it related to your sense of duty? Does it contain something you really enjoy doing as well? In other words, in which of

the shoulds is your heart involved? What do you care about and why do you care? Write it all down.

Day 3
Today you can download Alan Damron's song from Youtube, "Don't should on me and I won't should on you." (http://www.youtube. com/watch?v=nEBBpszMdPM). Listen to it often. Then begin to eval- uate what truly MUST be done, and what can be put off. You may well have to do the MUSTS first, but now you can function with a more thoughtful attention on how you feel and what you need for yourself while doing them.

Day 4
By now you may begin to suspect that there is another way of doing things, one that shows more respect for your physical and mental health. One aspect of the nervous system is geared to rev us up so we can deal with what's in front of us; another helps us cool down from the stresses of life. But in the modern world people spend most of their waking hours pushing themselves around, and seldom give themselves a breather. Experiment today with changing that proportion by introducing small interruptions and breathing breaks: Can you bring the ratio down from 80%–20% to 60%–40%? How does that affect your day?

Day 5
The pressures of life can be tyrannical in their demands on your body. Deadlines or requirements can drive you to even greater efforts, usually much faster than the body can move. But look at it this way: the head and body are separated by a bridge called the neck. Notice your head/neck/spine relationship right now. Is your head free to balance lightly on the spine or is your neck tense as your head hangs forward or pulls back and down? Even though it's a bridge, the neck often acts more like a wall that separates our head brain from the rest of us. Any tension in the neck interferes with the never-ending dialogue between the body and the brain. Notice frequently today how stress tightens your neck. Invite a release of your head off the spine to bring the shoulds in your life under your conscious attention. Any release of tension as you allow a full breath will activate your neck-bridge, allowing energy to flow between mind and body as it breaks through the wall that keeps you from being more wholly connected to your Self.

Too Busy to Live?

Isn't it a shame we're so busy. And yet the world's work must get done. If I close my eyes I can imagine all the people in this great city like tiny lights moving around town or in their apartments, meeting the needs of their lives. Some lights dance along subway platforms or wait in bus lines on their way to work, then sit in offices, visible yet invisible through the windows of skyscrapers (for who really bothers to look in?) Other lights move through the streets taking children to school or park, or weaving in and out of local stores. At the end of the day they all come home and turn on the lights, perhaps without realizing that they themselves carry a light inside.

Each of us has a light inside. The Quakers know it. As children we all knew it. It lit up everything we did with interest, excitement, and sometimes terror. But as we grow up the light seems to dim or disappear. In any case we are seldom aware of it unless we wonder from time to time what turned it off.

But even if that light has been forgotten, the equipment — the circuit, the wiring and the source — are still there. It may even shine forth once in a while when we stop to ask big questions, or when something stops us in our tracks. However, generally we're too busy to plug our attention into that current and light up what we're doing with the radiance of our own Being.

Remember the tale of the Robe of Glory and the boy who goes down into the dark of Egypt on a mission for his father, the King? Like us, he goes to sleep in the land of Everyday and forgets all that he was meant to be. Finally he wakes up and, with a lot of help from the world of Nature, obtains the Pearl he came for and heads back to his own country. As he nears home, he sees the Robe of Glory approaching him. When we waken, and turn toward it, it comes toward us.

As I read that story again the other day, my eyes welled up with tears. We are all children of a King and Queen, destined to inherit our own country if only we can remember who we are. In order to do that, we need to leave the castle of our father, the King, and find our own way in life's foreign country. It's part of growing up and becoming ourselves.

But what if that inner kingdom is calling us all day long and we never tune into its frequency? Must we always forget where we came from? Do we have to put that precious side of our life to sleep while we busy ourselves with the byplay of power and necessity? I need to work, to pay for a roof overhead, and food and clothing for myself and my dear ones. But am I too busy doing stuff to allow that inner light to shine?

If you sit quietly for a moment, you may become aware of the presence of another energy in you, in all of us, that we could call the energy of Being. It's different from the Doing energy of activity. Both of them are always present in us but our attention is habitually turned toward the one that calls us to action in the outer world. This week, take a few minutes every day just to sit with this thought: "I have two energies in me, and perhaps both are calling me, but I'm invested in one and seldom listen to the other." Then write out and prop up on your desk F. M. Alexander's adage: "No matter how many specific ends you may gain, you are worse off than before if in the process of gaining them you have destroyed the integrity of the organism." That organism is the home of your Self.

Day 1

Hurrying expresses a wish to be in the future because I think I'm late. It speeds me away from the present moment I'm living through. Master Alexander teacher Walter Carrington told his students to repeat each time, before they begin an action: "I have time." It calls on the nervous system to inhibit rushing forward under the neuro-physical command to "do it now!" at whatever cost. Try it today. Say it out loud. Send yourself a message to delay action for a nano-second, before jumping into the fray.

Day 2

Light a candle this morning as you introduce a momentary pause in your doings to sit quietly. Focus on it as it burns to keep your mind from running through the needs and desires of the coming day. Instead, concentrate your attention on the flame and on the energy inside you, the flame of your own Being. Try this for a short time, and then return to your life. As you go into your day, keep the candle's flickering flame in your mind's eye.

Day 3

Sitting still can be a powerful reorganizer of your energy in body, mind and heart. We tend to pour ourselves outward, drawn by everything we see, or spend time obsessing on past and future. The discipline of keeping the body quiet and your thoughts focused on the candle helps detach you briefly from the outer world, which attracts your attention like a great magnet. Yet, truly, there is another world within, if you allow it to appear. Sit still several times today, wherever you happen to be, and visualize your Self sitting in front of the candle.

Day 4

If your thoughts and imagination carry you away from the precise moment when you wish to be present to your Self, put on some music and follow the voice and instruments attentively with your thought. At the same time, keep a good part of your attention on your physical presence — the sensation of your body sitting there, butt on the chair or cushion, feet on the floor. Or if your mind won't stop interrupting your intention, count to 100 and back. That will draw it into quiet activity so it doesn't spirit you off to Timbuktu.

Day 5

Finally, the Royal Road to practicing your own presence is through paying attention to your breathing. As you follow it, your attention becomes engaged with body and mind simultaneously, inviting a new feeling of your Self to appear. Breathing exercises take many forms. Do some research and experiment with whatever method works best for you. One Zen practice is to count from one to five with each inbreath and outbreath as you bring your wandering thoughts again and again back to the sensation of your breathing Being.

In Praise of Questions

Somebody called me the other morning with a life-question I didn't know how to answer. The rest of my day centered around an active search in mind and heart as I went about my affairs. That led me to realize once again that our questions are often more valuable than our answers. They invite us to pause and re-examine our knowledge and experience and discard past solutions that may have once worked for us.

But here's the problem: when a question is raised, the mind, often left untenanted by our conscious awareness, immediately offers up any old tag for an answer. Gurdjieff compares our automatic, associative mind to a poorly trained secretary who files away formulations like labels, then pulls them out to fit any occasion. Such automatic responses are usually made up of what we've read, heard or remembered from the past. They don't necessarily fit life as we live it and seldom satisfy our need for understanding.

Life is constantly in movement. It is large, demanding, ever changing and re-forming, and tends to erupt vigorously with a new and unknown combination of circumstances. Labels, on the other hand, are local patches that pop up unconsciously and are stuck onto one small corner of what's going on, seldom related to the reality of our lives. We have needs we are forced to meet right now, head on, with our best intelligence. What use are labels for that?

What's more, answers can squeeze the juice out of a question without pouring any balm on the fire of our suffering. Only questions help us see things in a different way. They open new doors in mind and feeling, soothe a fevered state, or help us face what seems unbearable, even incomprehensible. While questions can be startling, confusing, and stir up our pain, they often lead to clarity or at least a new approach to an old problem. They stimulate consciousness. As soon as I realize I truly don't have an answer, I become quiet and aware, living the question with an uncertainty that demands all my attention. And attention itself, as Michel de Salzmann pointed out in his article on *Man's Ever New and Eternal Challenge*, is, "in its active form . . . in its purity, an act of questioning."

So while answers can make us feel better and allow us to think we've solved or disposed of problems, let's dare to sing the praises of questions, whether they come from outside or inside us. Uncomfortable though it may be to admit that I don't know, I become open to new dimensions in my Self and in the world.

Here's the rub: while a state of "total questioning in our living is the key to being," according to Michel de Salzmann, he also reminds us that there will always be resistance. We are so busy finding answers — and that's what we were brought up to do — that it's hard to keep ourselves open to questions. What's more, we are afraid of seeming stupid to ourselves or others if we don't have an immediate answer to any question.

Day 1

So why not take the challenge? Dare this very day to avoid all answers. Stutter, equivocate, refuse solutions, stir up questioning, ask yourself what alternatives might exist to every affirmation you meet, inner and outer, as you go through the day.

Day 2

A question can give form to the unnamable or bring you back to basics. Choose the latter as you go out into the world today. Operate like a journalist in pursuit of a story. Before making up your mind about anything, ask first: Who? What? Where? When? And, above all, Why? Bring such questions front and center into your day as you probe behind the surface meaning of things that happen, actions people take, and ideas they put forward.

Day 3

Small children are as full of questions as they are full of life. They see things freshly, and everything they see awakens interrogation. Today, experiment with a child's eye view of what's going on in your life. Take nothing for granted. Bring curiosity to each encounter and every situation that offers itself to you. Dig deeper.

Day 4

Today your focus could be less on queries about what's in front of you and more on exploring your own motives and inner explanations for everything you do. Our minds provide an automatic superficial explanation or excuse for our actions that may not have much to do with the underlying truth of why we think what we think and do what we do. Begin to explore your reasoning. Why are you doing whatever you are involved in at any moment? Don't forget to write down some of the automatic explanations that surge up right away. You'll probably hear them again.

Day 5

As Michel de Salzmann said above, questioning can awaken a subtler level of attention. Today you might take one of your discoveries from yesterday. For example, perhaps you noticed a repeated explanation you gave yourself that didn't quite get to the truth of your deeper motivations, or perhaps an unfriendly thought about someone else seemed to repeat itself a lot. See if you can uncover where it came from. Why is it sitting there in the storage closet of your mind, ready to pop out and attach itself to whatever comes along?

Love and Power

Everyone seems to be looking for power in one form or another. Power makes money and money is power. But love of power isn't limited to the world of business or politics. It exists in the world of illness and recovery as well. Therapists in the helping professions must acknowledge the attraction of power over others, even while attending to those in need. That means even if I'm one of the good guys, it's important for me to ask whether helping someone else is my way of reaffirming my right to occupy a corner of our planet.

Like many others, I was brought up to assume that things are either good or bad, true or false; that I'm either happy or miserable, lovable or hateful. However, it's never that simple. When you examine the power issue and see more deeply into your inner drives and defenses, as well as those of people around you, you'll discover, as I did, that the choices we are faced with aren't all black and white. We want to be good but our efforts can have bad effects; there's often falsehood mixed in with truth; we want and don't want whatever is our current desire.

Look at two of the primary human drives, love and power. Perhaps the opposite of love is not hate, which is always tinged with other emotions. Perhaps the opposite of love is power. Love accepts and embraces. Power refuses and crushes opposition. Love is kind and knows how to forgive, while power competes and takes others into account only when it stands in the Winner's Circle. And, as we all know, power corrupts.

But what's most disturbing is that both the need for power and the longing for love exist within me at the same time. Power is about dominating, owning, controlling, running the show; while love is about caring, taking in the message, finding what's needed, seeing what wishes to appear and helping it to flower. Yet, if I'm honest, both live in me — and you. There can be a drive for power behind the caring, helpful person or the one who wants only to please, as well as the take-charge kind of guy. Let's face it. We are all lovers in love with love but also in love with power. Perhaps Martin Buber said it best:

"Do not protest: 'Let love alone rule!'
Can you prove it true?
But resolve: every morning I shall concern myself anew
About the boundary between the love-deed — Yes
And the power-deed — No
And pressing forward honor reality."

In the first chapter of **Meetings With Remarkable Men** *there's an aphorism Gurdjieff's father often used about relationships between people: "I am up because you are down." In the light of that saying, you might want to investigate the ego's incessant need for power and control by studying the motives behind your actions and reactions.*

Day 1
The need to feel powerful often veils fear or a sense of lurking danger. Today study the power plays between you and people you meet and exchange with during the day. See if you can discover whether there's a hidden motive on either side, or a hidden fear. Can you figure out whether you stand on a higher or lower rung of the Power Ladder in any given situation?

Day 2
On the other hand, the ego can be very suggestible when it doesn't need shoring up. At such times, we may give ourselves away too easily to a cause or an avatar. We often cede power to others when we feel unsure of ourselves, because we don't know how to maintain our own ground — unable to defend ourselves from their intrusion. Maybe it's a lack of energy at that moment, or a lack of clarity just then. Try to notice today, when do you give up power, perhaps to avoid conflict?

Day 3
When you've gathered enough data on the ego's need for power as well as how we give up our power and individuality in small ways, you might want to investigate a subject politicians and historians have studied for

centuries: the principle of the Balance of Power. Read up on it, then ask yourself, "What's needed, at any moment, to restore my own personal inner Balance of Power?" Spend today with that question.

Day 4
Each of us, whether or not we are in a position of power over others, needs to separate the strands of our imaginary authority, our ego image, from the authority of a higher intelligence that we share with the universe. That power of intelligent thought, sweet reason, is never mine. It's always on loan, like my life. While accessing it depends on the state I'm in, it's a continually renewable resource. Where does your true authority lie? Write down your thoughts.

Day 5
Krishnamurti said that the violence, the negativity, the caring and the possibility of balance exist in everyone at any moment, reminding us that, "You are the world." Seek balance now, not later. While you may wish to serve the greater good, there's a legitimate need for self-affirmation, which can be confused with the relentless drive for power and success. When does this apply to you or to the person you are speaking with? How to be present in the midst of all your opposing tendencies? A real understanding of this issue could lead you to a radically new point of view: that the power is in the service not the person.

Returning again to Buber:

> "We cannot avoid using power,
> Cannot escape the compulsion
> To afflict the world.
> So let us, cautious in diction
> And mighty in contradiction,
> Love powerfully."

Dare To Be Present

Sounds strange? Aren't we mostly there? Not at all! We avoid connecting with a deeper level in ourselves all the time, and I suspect there's a good reason for it.

When I tried a few minutes ago to be right here in the present moment, I was surprised by the number of inner barriers to the attempt. Lots of things on my to-do list, for one thing. My mind was hankering to go on planning for the day, but I intentionally cut that off and sat still then and there. A minute later I recalled a disagreement with a family member and began to relive it, muttering how I should have said or done this or that. "Let go," I told myself firmly, turning back to the present moment, and soon found I was planning the day again. There was too much on my plate!

"Enough of this wandering mind!" I cried, at first to no avail. However, as soon as I turned my attention to the state of my body, my head brain became quieter. I began to relax as I took in physical complaints I hadn't noticed before: a slight soreness in the left hip, an ache in the middle of my back. Not big things, just there, part of me. In any case, I don't want to know about them if I can avoid it.

Whoa! That's a major barrier. And there's more: not only do I not want to feel my aches and pains, I'm also often annoyed by them. The unconscious attitude I uncovered at that moment was, "What right have they to interfere with what I'm doing?" Say hullo to my reactive nature, the emotional life that flows on in me 24/7. It never stops, and along with my turning thoughts, it drowns out whatever else is going on. And if I'm mildly depressed or irritated or anxious, it's happening below the radar of my conscious life. Only when I feel something strongly — anger, fear, joy, jealousy — do I notice my emotions. Yet mild or strong, whatever emotion is king of my inner castle creates a lot of static in my system.

So even as I try to be quietly attentive to the present moment, parts of me seem determined to interfere. Each thought, ache, or reaction calls my attention away from the experience of "now." And here's the clincher: I often don't even *want* to know what's really going on because it makes me feel uncomfortable about myself. I don't want to acknowledge how hard it is to be present, or how often I fail. Why should I admit I'm such a loser!

So I issue this challenge to us all: *dare* to be present. It's not easy. You may have to accept confusion, anxiety, and minor aches and pains when you try. You may have to admit that you're off-balance and confess, "I'm not where I want to be." Or, "I'm not happy right this minute." That's so not pleasant! And none of us wants to feel that way. Yet, oh how much we long to be present to our true Self, and to life.

What can give you the courage to stay here, seeing what is, listening to the conflicting voices inside, until all the aspects of your inner world reorganize into their rightful places? How to activate the intelligence of the mind simultaneously with the reality of body and feeling, so that new perceptions can appear? **Be Here Now:** *those three little words make it sound so simple. But the act is anything but easy because, when you think about it, for such an experience to be possible, three worlds need to relate to each other in you.*

Day 1
Experiment with this today. First, check up on the state of tension in your body, the house of your Being. Do this as often as possible by turning all your attention for a few minutes to scan your body parts, one by one. From time to time, throughout the day, sense how your feet touch the floor when you stand and walk, or notice your butt on the chair whenever you sit. As you do it, ask yourself, "do I want to be here right now?" Give an honest answer. You may not always want to be where you are but you are choosing to connect with what's real.

Day 2
When being in the present isn't so comfortable, remind yourself of those special moments of presence you've experienced in the past. They serve as a kind of proof that, when the ego calms down, the head and emotions

become quiet, and your container, the body, offers its here-and-now kinesthetic message, you feel more alive.

Day 3

What to call that life that resonates with a sensation of oneself? Energy or chi or prana are words used to describe it, but it's much more than a thought. Tune in quietly today to see if you can capture a three-dimensional experience of your Self: the blood coursing in its channels through muscle and around bone in a continuing dialogue between the body and the brain. And, at the center, the breathing being that you are. When you focus on the breath, try to follow its movement all the way from your belly through chest and back, up to the arms and shoulders. Even your head rides on the breath. Every bit of you moves with the breathing.

Day 4

You have accounted for two worlds when body and mind come together in the sensation of yourself. Now it's time to be Here, at the center of your Self, in your room or office or wherever you are. The room reflects your small world, filled with possessions and memories. Around you are colleagues or neighbors, in their private worlds. Beyond them are streets or parks or fields, whole neighborhoods in the city, state, country, world you live in. And all of it lives within the embrace of the universe in which our small planet rotates. So, as you stand or sit or move around today, visualize yourself centered in this larger world.

Day 5

Today, turn your mind often in search of the sensation of your Self as you acknowledge your only reality: this moment in time. Life may often seem like a horizontal race over barriers to a perceived or mysterious goal, but Now is not a horizontal line. Rather, its most accurate symbol is the cross, at the center of which is this vertical moment that connects me with eternity. Place yourself often in that center today and say, "I am here because I choose to be here, to be my whole Self at this moment in time." And as you move beyond time into the timeless present, say out loud, "I am here now."

The Blame Game

Some say the world is divided into two kinds of people — those who attack, complain and even rage against what life is serving them up, and those with a victim mentality, as in "life is cruel" and "poor little me." Much depends on how our parents treated us and the events in our past, but it's always fruitful to examine how we receive the life we've been given.

Perhaps the most pernicious form of blaming is the kind we turn on ourselves. Do you look over your own shoulder as you go about your day and scold yourself when you catch yourself being rude or inconsiderate or forgetful? I do. There's a critic in me always on the lookout for when I fall short of how I think I ought to be at any given moment. He calls me stupid or insensitive.

And I suppose a certain amount of self appraisal is ok, up to a point. After all, we seek to be decent, productive people and realize that some aspects of ourselves may pull in opposing directions. But there's a limit, a boundary that we all need to know better. Because if that inner critic attacks almost every gesture we make, almost every thought we think, then he's working too hard and we're getting too much grief!

So why attack ourselves at all? And perhaps a more important question is, could we live free of the Blame Game? There's an encouraging message in the *I Ching: or Book of Changes*, where the words "no blame" are repeated many times, under many different circumstances.

For example, Hexagram 14, "Possession in Great Measure," says that although great possessions attract danger, whether or not one is able to protect them, "If one remains conscious of difficulty, one remains without blame." Or take Hexagram 17, "Following," which states that it doesn't matter whether what we intend works out the way we think it should as long as we do our best, because

"Perseverance furthers. No blame." I hope everyone hears that! No matter what problems or difficulties we do or do not overcome, there's no blame. What a relief!

Rather than blame yourself for anything, imagine a forgetful or naughty child. To teach her how to mend her ways you wouldn't pour on her the kind of criticism or sarcasm you probably dump on yourself, would you? Of course not! You'd take her by the hand, sit her down and explain in some way what's missing from her world-view. And you would probably have to repeat the message many times — lovingly — before it becomes a part of that child's understanding. Talk to yourself in the same gentle way.

Self-accusation short-circuits our true feelings. It builds on the assumption that we are probably always wrong, that there's no way to live up to the perfection to which we aspire. Perhaps you'd find it useful to pull out Marion Woodman's Addiction to Perfection *and study the Inner Judge in each of us — the Wicked Witch who loves to tear down rather than build up the psyche.*

Day 1
Notice all through the day, and write down as often as you can, each passing thought of blaming: What do you blame yourself or others for? As you dare to go deeper into this self-examination — often neglected because it seems so right to criticize oneself — you may make a surprising discovery. What seems to be an appropriate inner correction just might be an unconscious inflation. Ask yourself, who is this Perfect Person you're supposed to be? Does she or he even exist on earth? What mortal would be capable of such perfection?

Day 2
Today try to accept the conditions you are in. Receive the impression of whatever happens rather than criticize. Focus all your energy on being alert, without wasting time in complaint or accusation. In Lizelle Reymond's book, To Live Within, *Sri Anirvan offers an attitude that might be helpful here: "Man is at the same time the cat that eats the mouse and the mouse devoured by the cat, for these are the two ways in which life comes toward us." So at what moments are you the cat and when the mouse?*

Day 3

In order to avoid both criticism and self-pity, it's important to become inwardly more active. As you face each challenging situation today, inquire into the practical possibilities available to you. What would it take for you to look more carefully at what's really going on, learning to embrace whatever happens, trying to choose better or take more time before making assumptions and leaping into reactions?

Day 4

Here's some key information from the commentary to The Gospel of Mary Magdalene, *translated by Jean-Yves Leloup: "It is not we who make the path; it is we who give it direction. This is our true power." That means you have some power. Use it well today as you attempt to steer your earthly vehicle. Remind yourself of the direction in which you truly wish to go and ask yourself how to adapt the circumstances you are in so that you can gradually move towards it, no matter how difficult they may be.*

Day 5

The text goes on to say: "Perhaps the world has no meaning in itself — it is given to us to discover one. This of course requires courage. But more than anything else, it requires imagination — that sublime imagination that may be glimpsed in certain thoughts hastily dismissed as crazy by those who ignore them, or heard in certain poems, in certain angelic messages . . . and in all of the great sacred texts." That means help is available. It's out there. What will you do to connect with it today?

What Weighs Us Down?

This morning my Yoga teacher said that the two main things that weigh us down are gravity and expectation. Gravity? Sure — an inexorable law. But expectation? That's harder to figure out, because I like to look forward to things. So I asked myself, "if I'm trudging through my day with the world on my shoulders, is it because I expected so much more than I'm getting? Are things not turning out the way I'd hoped they would?"

How well I remember the high school parties of my wallflower youth, when it seemed as though hoping to have a good time destroyed its possibility. After the first few evenings of total disappointment, I determined quite young to pull back. "Never look forward to a party," I ordered myself. "That way if you have fun it will be a nice surprise."

However, I soon discovered that giving up expectations was harder than I thought. Remember the story of the Zen master who came to a river on his way to a temple and walked across it? When his disciple begged to know how to walk on water, the master assured him it was easy: "As you step off the riverbank," he said, "just do not think of elephants." But, like elephants, we can't forget.

Expectation is in the background of everything we undertake. Who would bother to go through four years of college without expecting a degree? Who would invest in a stock without expecting to make money? Who would call for help without thinking someone might come? But perhaps you've already noticed a subtle difference among these examples. At college, I expected to work for good marks, and knew I could flunk out, so it was a reasonable assumption that if I did the work I'd graduate. As for investing in the stock market, any assumption is unreasonable — I'd better believe I'm taking a gamble, even if the stock is highly recommended by experts.

And how about a call for help? Most help is conditional — it comes at a price. For example, I have a right to ask for help of the computer company, the refrigerator man, the plumber. And they have a right to get paid or, if the machinery was faulty, a duty to make our bargain whole. But in time of real need, help can come to us in the form of grace, reaching us where we are most helpless. I've found that, in such cases, what's important is to give up any expectation. When I can go on no longer, I acknowledge my ignorance, my inability, my helplessness, and open to the unknown. That's when help comes.

Although we may need help, we are often too full of ourselves to receive it, weighted down by what's going on in our lives. Thoughts whirl, emotional reactions jump, the body makes its demands, even as we long to clear all the inner noise away to be quiet and aware. Here's an analogy you can call to mind and heart every day this week when you need to quiet the inner hubbub.

Step 1
Imagine a river stirred up by a storm — a big one. Once it's gone, all the detritus from the riverbank floats along on the surface with bits of trees and bushes. The river itself is brown and thick with sediment from top to bottom. Not an inch of clear water. That image might apply to a stormy reaction or a moment of confusion in your day.

Step 2
Then imagine that the sun comes out. There's no wind, just a gentle breeze that kisses your face. Slowly, slowly, you watch the detritus float away down the river as the sediment sinks to the bottom, and the waters become clear and still. The quiet undercurrent flows on. Just so, when you sit down to bring reason to your confusion, you can imagine that a river runs through you. As Deepak Chopra pointed out in Quantum Healing: *"The material body is a river of atoms, the mind is a river of thought, and what holds them together is a river of intelligence."*

Step 3
To find that clear, peaceful river inside, it's helpful first to recognize all that's been stirred up in you. Sometimes the whole body feels choked with weeds or sediment and there's no free space anywhere. But if you watch

how your thoughts shift endlessly like clouds across the deep blue of the sky, you can begin to separate from them. You are the sky, not the clouds. Hopefully your head will gradually empty as you invite the sediment of turning thoughts to sink down into your chest. That takes time, so give it time.

Step 4
The chest, seat of our emotional life, harbors any number of storms. So when your inner weather is stormy, full of sorrow, outrage, anxiety, annoyance, begin to pay attention to whatever is going on there. As you listen to these inner sobs, mutterings and arguments, focus on the fact that that they aren't out there in the world, opposing you. They are inside you. Yes, they may weigh you down, but they aren't you. Once your heart realizes there's a listener attending to its complaints, it may find solace. Sooner or later, as you wait and listen, your chest will empty its burden as the whirling sediment of thoughts and emotions sinks down into the belly. Then you may begin to feel more like yourself and less like a storm at sea.

Step 5
Perhaps the belly is where all those reactions belong. As you sit there and continue to listen, compare the bottom of your torso to the bottom of a river. Or if you are standing, connect your mind with your feet as they sink into the ground. Bottom or feet, that's where the sediment can mass and give weight to your life. You need weight to stay firmly on the planet rather than float around in space like an astronaut. Let the law of gravity offer you clear waters above and solid mass below. In stormy or even fair weather, as you stand and sit and move around, remind yourself often that a river runs through you.

Leaping the Barrier

There's often a barrier between how I am — busy me in the middle of my life — and the way I'd like to be with others: open and attentive. That's because, when I'm in my Executive Mode, I'm usually driven by a series of problems to solve or a deadline to meet. There's not much room left for listening or feeling.

But without listening or feeling, who am I? Surely not the whole person I wish to be. Yes, I may feel directed, active, engaged in life. But a precious piece of myself is missing — the part that can take in and give value to what's going on. Your situation may well be like mine, since it's almost endemic amid the demands of our busy world. The fact is, when I'm rushing along on the surface of my life, I'm like a machine in which the automatic functioning of thoughts and emotional reactions sets the pace. How to reduce the robotic speed that keeps me from processing what's really going on?

Sometimes the only solution is to come to a complete stop. That way I can begin again from a different place. But it's not easy because, like any object in motion, my machinery wants to stay in motion. And I've learned from experience that if I don't engage actively in slowing it down, the 'high' of busyness won't come to an end till I'm exhausted. How to shift out of overdrive before I try to put on the brakes?

Perhaps I really wish to be open to someone or engage more deeply in what I'm doing at the moment. Nevertheless, it's hard to let go of the tendency to speed up when I'm too directed, too intent, too closed to other influences. So recently I've begun to practice a new exercise. First I tell myself firmly not to move so quickly on to the next thing. Then I visualize driving down a narrow country road with a wooden fence on one side, and a beautiful open field beyond it. That's probably Rumi's field, the one "beyond right doing and wrong doing." If I'm truly tired of driving myself grimly onward, I sincerely want to move into that open field.

O.K. It's time to stop the car and somehow clamber over the fence. I get out of the car, and plant myself in front of the fence, saying bluntly to myself: "There's no alternative. If you want to live in another way you've got to make the leap." Hesitantly at first, I put one foot over the other to climb awkwardly up the wooden rungs. (Who can look graceful scrambling over a country fence?)

Then comes the hardest part. I sit at the top, looking down on that lovely meadow, but to get to it I'll have to jump. What will I land in? Cornfield stubble, sharp as thorns? Cow dung? Will the attempt bring pain or remorse? Maybe it will, but if I'm able to make the leap, I'm usually glad I did. Reality is on the other side.

Making the leap has always been difficult for me, perhaps for you, too. Here's why: if I choose to be open, I must accept to be vulnerable. That takes courage, plus enough energy to cope with whatever may follow. One side of me wants to dare while another side shrinks away, wanting to keep to the known path to avoid the risk of being hurt. If this is true for you, you may need to bring your earthly vehicle to a complete stop in order to change gears. You are moving from a mechanical operation to attempting to be conscious. Think of it as putting a spanner in a turning wheel.

Day 1
Stopping cold provides your automatic pilot with a small shock. You can do it with as simple a question as "Hey, wait a minute! What's going on here?" Try asking that question every now and then today. Or find your own Stop-the-World query.

Day 2
Today, it's time for another question: "What do I really want?" Yes, maybe you have to keep on doing whatever your work in life is. We usually do. But it's worth examining not the why of it, but how you are doing it. Is your mind relaxed and open to adapt instantly to new circumstances? Is your body moving freely in space? Or not? Write down your discoveries.

Day 3

You've already questioned both what you are doing and how you are doing it. Now make a list of alternative choices for what you really want in life and for how you would like to relate to your work and your colleagues. Try out a few of these choices during the day and write down what happens. You'll find it's not so easy but perhaps well worth the attempt. Tonight, as you read your notes and listen to your inner reactions and responses, ask yourself "What does my heart want?"

Day 4

Today you might put in place some small alternative action to replace whatever habitual drive you've begun to question. When you do, it's important to recognize that every time you attempt something new, resistance will automatically appear. Don't be discouraged. Resistance is lawful. Each time you make a new effort there will be opposition, criticism and doubt, because part of you wants to stay in the status quo. It's more comfortable.

Day 5

With awareness of your new direction and recognition of the resistance that opposes it, you are ready to act, to make the leap, to take the risk without knowing what you will land in. As you attempt to bring a new approach to an automatic activity, don't expect miracles, but experiment again and again, for a few minutes each time, throughout the day. You've heard the Chinese maxim that the thousand-mile journey always begins with the first step? So keep in mind: no step, no journey.

Why Switch Partners?
Grow Together

I just heard it for the hundredth time. A friend said to me yesterday with a deep sigh, "people just don't change." He then confided that he had spent months trying to please his new partner. Don't we all feel that way from time to time? "If only so-and-so could be different, we could have a real relationship. She/he just doesn't understand . . . " usually followed by a long list of corrections we'd be glad to share in order to rehabilitate him or her to our way of thinking or doing.

Why are we so determined to change each other and ourselves? I confess I've spent a lot of the time of my life trying to make myself over as well as dedicating time to help others try to reinvent themselves. But now I see it differently. So when my friend baldly stated his disillusionment, images of a few unusual people immediately popped into my mind. They had learned how to make conscious choices, whether pursuing studies in science, philosophy, psychology or the spiritual life. Rather than focus on making themselves over from the outside, they worked at becoming aware of what was driving them deep inside.

It's not easy to catch a glimpse of the reality below the superficial explanations of why we do what we do and are how we are. But if you've already made many attempts to square your particular circle, why not experiment with a new attitude? Instead of working to change yourself and others, work at enlarging your definition of what a relationship is. Spontaneous attraction may be celebrated in story and song, but the reality is that good relationships are made, not born.

So here's the challenge: I, you, we, they can grow. As we uncover aspects of ourselves and others that we do or don't like, we can opt for a larger worldview — to accept what is, rather than judge it. That provides us with a new question to ask ourselves or our partner. Not "how can I change you to think or feel or act the way I want you to?" but "how can I help you change into yourself?" In other words, how can we help each other grow?

If you can't 'change' someone else, you can at least begin to know yourself better. Are you and your partner always coming at each other with the same criticisms? "Leaves the seat up, smokes in the house, doesn't put away the dishes, doesn't listen, doesn't understand me." Some of us employ a particular tone of voice that tells others we think they're way off base, so they always feel judged. Any of us can trigger a customary dust-up. And like a doctor who prescribes medication to eliminate the symptoms, we often engage in superficial makeovers under the heading of How Not to Rock the Boat.

Day 1

Take a closer look at your own particular merry-go-round today. Will it ever come to a stop? Review in your mind any emotional frustrations between you and your near and dear ones in the last week or month. Do the same disagreements come up again and again? Why is that? Is there a key issue hidden under the immediate reactions? Could fear be a factor? Or desperation to maintain the status quo? Write down your thoughts and guesses.

Day 2

Today investigate who began the latest unpleasant encounter, and what was going on before it started. Could there be a misunderstood point of view at its heart? Could a little straight talk refocus the problem? Once reactions quiet down and two intelligent people look at the same event, honesty can clear the air. Why not reduce any long-term emotional static after the storm has passed? Study one recent incident with a microscope, and if you feel up to it, discuss it with your friend.

Day 3

Make a general examination of what words or actions of others trigger reactions in you. Once you've written them down, ask yourself whether you do or say any of those things yourself. Often what we react to in others is related to something we also do unconsciously. Psychologists call it projection. I project onto the other guy the thought or action I dislike in myself. Be alert to any sentence that starts, "I just can't stand . . . "

Day 4

What would be the ideal relationship with your partner? Write down the qualities you'd like your dream partner to have on one side of the page, adding a star to whichever of them the real person already has. On the other side, write down what you think your own good qualities are. What's good enough for you in her or him? What in yourself is worthy of enhancing the life of your partner? What do both of you value most? Can you celebrate what you both value and condone what bothers you in each other?

Day 5

The most important effort in understanding your relationships is to acknowledge how subjective your reactions and complaints are. What can you learn from your partner? How can the differences between you teach you more about life? My husband was my opposite in many ways, very Latin, very self-involved, somewhat passive-aggressive. But he shared many interests and passions with me, and his fearlessness in the face of other people's emotional tirades gave me courage. What did I learn? That every moment you accept yourself as you are and the other as he is brings the relationship to a deeper level.

Are You a Leader or a Follower?

One little appreciated path to consciousness is the practice of following. You might think it sounds easy. Isn't it a lot harder to lead, to stay ahead of the crowd, as many of us have to do in our work, than just to follow along? But because many of us are busily engaged for most of our waking hours in running our own show — getting ahead on the job, taking care of the family, it's habitual for us to be in charge. So even in the early morning, when I dedicate myself to Tai Chi and meditation, I feel the pull toward getting on with my day.

Following is a pure form of inner exercise. Whether standing, sitting, or moving, when we follow we give up pushing ourselves, our world, and other people around. Instead of *doing* something, we participate in whatever is going on. Following also helps quiet the confusion inside.

Mind/body practices like Yoga or Tai Chi teach us how to follow. They calm the emotions, focus the mind, and strengthen the immune system, promoting health and balance through mindful awareness of oneself in movement. In a very real sense, they help us stay younger and healthier as we grow older. And they are all about following, not leading.

A consummate doer, I often get into a put-your-head-down-and-go attitude, grimly determined to finish at all costs whatever I'm involved in. When I wake up to the fact that I'm driving myself, I try to practice *following*. First I give up whatever I'm engaged in for a minute or two as I call up the memory of the morning's Tai Chi exercise. That ushers in a deeper breath. "Let go!" I tell myself. Then, as I go back to work, I invite my mind to follow carefully every movement I make in the next few minutes of my life.

To lead or to follow? Each has its place in our lives. And the choice is always up to us. Life and *chi* flow through us in a river of energy. We can spend time longing to swim while stranded on the bank, or bob on the surface of the water like flotsam. But as we pay attention to ourselves in the present moment, relinquishing expectations, we begin to discover advantages even in the difficulties we face. And — perhaps most important — as we follow along, giving up knowing what's going to happen next, we enter a state of availability, ready for anything.

The legendary Taoist, Zhang Sanfeng, was said to have originated the first Tai Chi movements after watching the dance between a snake and a bird as they attacked each other in turn and then retreated to defend themselves. One of his sayings was: "In resting be as still as a mountain and in movement, be like a river." It's that river-like flow of chi that frees you to follow your own movements, internal and external, rather than push yourself around.

Day 1

Today, while you are engaged in your activities, check in at any time to find out whether your attitude at that moment is that of a leader or a follower. Notice when you lose your connection with the natural flow of your energy and automatically start pushing yourself or others around. Are your actions based on an exchange of force and resistance, or can you allow what needs to be done to happen, as you shape and accompany it? Are you able to stop pushing and participate in whatever's going on?

Day 2

Follow the relationship between your two hands. Are they aware of each other, turning and talking to each other as you move about and do things? My Tai Chi teacher, T. T. Liang, said they are "like one bird following another." Notice the exchange of energy between one hand and the other, as they move through space always in relation to each other. If you continue to follow them with your attention, they will soon become alive and tingling.

Day 3

You can also experience following by focusing on your legs — how do they work together as your weight shifts when while you walk? One leg leads, the other follows; one empties, the other fills with weight. Then it is reversed. When you stand still, let your mind energy filter down through you as your feet sink into the earth. As you walk, try imagining that the air you are moving through is heavier than water, and that you are swimming through it.

Day 4
Following can be helpful when you are emotionally upset or suffering from physical or mental distress. Whatever you have to accomplish today, whether working at the office or cooking or doing the laundry, concentrate all your attention on the very next move you are about to make and follow the energy as you go into action. Then allow your attention to pass on seamlessly as you follow your next movement.

Day 5
When you feel sorrow, outrage, anxiety, or annoyance, pay attention to it. Listen to all the inner murmurs as you try to accept that they are in you but not of you. In other words, you are the witness of what's going on, not the victim or the perpetrator. As you follow the inner complaint or suffering, it may begin to quiet down. Sooner or later the furor will sink deep into the belly as your energy returns once more to the Ocean of Chi — a storehouse located below the navel — where it can fertilize your future flowering.

Accentuating the Positive

"Give me a place to stand on," said the Greek mathematician Archimedes, "and I can move the world." He was talking about his invention of using pulleys and levers to raise very heavy objects. A physicist, engineer, inventor, and astronomer as well, Archimedes revolutionized geometry and anticipated Integral Calculus 2,000 years before Newton and Leibniz. But he was also a practical man who invented a wide variety of machines.

In the simplest sense, his statement is also true of our inner world of moods. When I feel anger, depression or any violent reaction coming on, I could look for a position on which I can take a stand while the storm passes through me. If I could leverage my inner world out of its momentary negative hell and back to ease and contentment, what a relief that would be!

The problem is, of course, how? Once a mood has reached its full flow of expression, it's almost impossible to change the direction of the energy that's pouring out of me. It has to play itself out, even if it leaves me aching, exhausted and, perhaps, apologetic. But here's where leveraging comes in: if I can bring conscious awareness to the negative reaction early enough, before it begins to take me over, and if I care enough not to waste myself on it, there's hope. The trick is to apply leverage before that small complaining stream becomes a raging river. That way, there's a good chance I can escape the worst of it.

Not that it's easy. For one thing, I have to sacrifice the positive enjoyment of being angry. Most people actually love to be angry. It gives them a sense of really being there, a kind of negative "I am." In a perverse way they feel fired up: "Look at me now! I'm enormous when I'm in a rage!" And of course there are many other negative emotions we cling to in different ways. For example, all of us are prone to being victims of self-pity, which cuts us off from our energy as it is sucked into a black hole of despair.

If we understood better the value of the energy that's wasted, we'd be more determined to leverage bad moods into good ones. Every morning we are given enough for the day, both the jet fuel of spirit and the ordinary psycho-physical gasoline that keeps our vehicle going. However, any violent outburst or negative feeling state I allow myself to affirm will lay waste to it. Gurdjieff said that a big burst of negativity can wipe out a whole day's energy and, if the eruption is strong enough, one could be depleted for a week, a year or even the rest of one's life. Ominous thought!

When you go to the gym or prepare for a serious run, you probably do a little stretching first. Your muscles need warming up and you take time out for that. How about exercising your psychic musculature to develop a subtler awareness of moods and flashpoints in order to be ready to leverage yourself out of your day's portion of negative emotions. Bad temper, impatience, irritation, despondency are habitual negative reactions that could be replaced with more positive feelings, but it's not easy. Here are some experiments you could try.

Day 1
In order to leverage yourself out of a negative reaction, place your attention somewhere specific. For example, stand up and focus on your psycho-physical presence right where you are now. We tend to hang our weight carelessly on one hip and leg or the other. Begin to stand consciously, weight evenly divided between your feet, as if each foot were in the palm of your hand and you were weighing yourself in your mind. Standing still and acknowledging your weight on the earth can give you a new sense of yourself here and now. You contain a lot of energy. Become aware of it moving through you. Energy is power. Don't give it away to any bad mood that comes along.

Day 2
Today, as soon as you notice rising anger at the nasty remark someone made, or sense a depressed or jealous feeling overtake you, concentrate on your weight on the ground. Here you stand. Imagine your roots growing down into the earth below as you stand on two equally supportive feet. Then shift your weight slowly from one foot to the other several times. Raise one foot slowly, balance there a moment, then put it down and raise the other. Call up an image of the dance of the Indian

god, Shiva, the Destroyer, with one foot high in the air while the other presses an ogre down into the earth. Press your bad mood down into the dust in the same way.

Day 3

Experiment today with altering some of your physical habits to learn how your organism reacts any time you attempt to change your behavior. For example, practice using your other hand today as you pour the coffee, answer the telephone, turn the key in the lock, or brush your teeth. As you challenge small physical habits in this way, it gives you a feel for the mechanisms involved when you attempt to shift away from more intractable emotional habits. You are not your habits, but your energy may be imprisoned in them.

Day 4

If you are a dedicated doer with a long laundry list of things you are determined to get through, you may frequently find yourself annoyed at anything or anyone who interferes with your forward motion. Today, each time you finish a task, come to a stop and wait a few moments before you move on to the next one. In that quiet space, ask yourself, "How am I feeling?" and "What is my body up to?" Whenever you become conscious of your grim determination to finish something at all costs, take a moment to stand still and receive the support of Mother Earth.

Day 5

Another day, when you feel the beginnings of anger, annoyance or impatience, enlarge your picture of yourself in your mind, step by step. Here you are, standing or sitting down, in your office or apartment, in your city and country. Remind yourself that you are one person in a world of more than seven billion human beings and a solar system of unimaginable proportions. If you were able to enlarge your vision step by step in this way, and even add in the Milky Way, surely that would blow a small, personal reaction out of anyone's mind!

Mind the Gap

Between knowing all that my head already grasps, which is considerable, and taking it in with my heart, there is a gap. "I think therefore I am," said the wise man. But how can the rest of me digest the events of my life, make sense of them and move on? Let's reverse Descartes' statement as follows: "I am, therefore I think, feel, sense and suffer." Because the fact is that whether or not the thinking part of me has explanations, I'm full of pain and (sometimes) joy but seldom understand the why of it all.

I suspect there may be someone in the deepest recesses of my mind who knows what I ought to have done or ought to be doing now. But although that someone may well see what's needed, the person I usually am doesn't seem able to act on it. I guess I need help.

That's important to recognize because, once acknowledged, it leads me to explore new solutions. I've already gone to the bookstore, where there are books on cooking or cancer or anger or grief. Problem is, real help doesn't necessarily appear by just thinking things over. Help seems to need three dimensions while thought has only two.

Thought turns everything into black or white, this or that, either/or, while our lives wear all the colors of the spectrum, often stained with the black of real tragedy or the deep purple of self-pity. In any case, as soon as I feel sorrow or outrage, my body tenses up, even as my head offers endless explanations about what I should or could say or do. But all the heart knows is that it is in pain.

Although I have often told myself that a painful experience is something to "get over," I'm now wondering whether that's just another escape hatch from reality. Whatever I'm going through is not something to be resolved so I can "get on with the rest of my life" because, in this moment, it *is* my life! How to find another way of looking at my situation?

I was pondering this on the London subway en route to a performance of *The Magic Flute* when, out of the blue, my bafflement was resolved. We had entered a great curving station where the exit doors are dangerously far from the edge of the platform. "MIND THE GAP," intoned the recorded voice of a bored Brit: "MIND THE GAP."

There it is, the missing link — the gap between the ideal and the present, the perfect and the contingent — between the head's unending supply of words as solutions and the heart's unending difficulties with absorbing the truth of the situation. This gap needs to be "minded." It needs to be filled with mind. Our job is to bring the mind's best attention to our active, caring psycho-physical presence, to fill the gap. In other words, be there.

"I am a part of all that I have met," said Tennyson, but the opposite also holds true. All that I have met is now a part of me. So whatever difficulty you face is part of your own story, a special dish served up to you by life, with ingredients culled from all that you've lived through, spiced by all the people you've listened to or turned away from.

Day 1
As a first step to minding the gap, try to take in impressions of what you might call "my way." Your personal point of view, your take on how to live, your way of doing things, your attitudes to life situations, perhaps different from anyone else's. Notice and write down your personal approach to every event, person and situation you find yourself in today.

Day 2
Now you can go deeper into discovering your habitual reactions and automatic solutions. Become alert to differences. Not everyone has the same point of view or attitude. How is yours different from that of other people you know? Do you usually think things out? Do you hate to make decisions? Do you react with startlement to anything new or do you tend to say, "I don't give a damn"? What acts of others do you take

personally? When do you insist they follow your way? What's your way of resolving issues or arguing your point of view?

Day 3

We share many experiences, pass through similar stages, are overcome by the same passions, espouse or deny the same values. But the gap is always there, between all the head sees and already grasps, and the taking it in, absorbing it, accepting it and living it as one's life. What is your life about? What do you stand for? What do you stand against? Write down what you think of as your deeper views and attitudes to the larger questions about the meaning of life. How are you living by them today?

Day 4

We use our mental machinery to think and notice, and it's essential to our functioning. But as you re-read yesterday's notes, you could engage in a deeper level of exploration, a search for understanding the meaning behind the thoughts. Gurdjieff's view was that knowledge is one thing and Being another, and that real understanding is the fruit of experiencing both together. So as you go through your day, see if you can bring how you feel about different situations you meet into contact with your explanations or judgments about them.

Day 5

You have three major functions — thinking, feeling and body consciousness. The possibility of being present to your life has to do with finding a place of balance in which they are related to each other, tuned into the larger whole of who you are. To do this, Gurdjieff suggested, "Think what you feel; feel what you think." What does that mean to you? Experiment with it today.

A Sense of Inadequacy

There is a level of reality on which we are nothing and we know it. A glance at the sky on a starry night reminds us of that fact. Standing in front of a towering mountain range confirms it. So does feeling incompetent when faced by "experts" in any field, or awkward in the presence of someone else's grace. And on a larger scale, we will always feel inadequate when faced with the suffering of our loved ones or the world's calamities.

But the word *inadequate* may not be accurate because each of us is someone: a person living for a brief moment under those starry skies, climbing that mountain for a little while. We are representatives of the human condition on earth with all its mental and emotional complexities and physical attributes. Yes, we are like particles of sand compared to the vastness of the universe, but without sand there would be no beach.

Then why do we so often feel inadequate to the task, to the relationship, or to getting ourselves into gear to do something that needs to be done? Suppose you couldn't quite figure something out or you didn't move as fast as you think you should. Or maybe you feel helpless, dependent and not "worth" anything because you're just plain tired. In any case, you may be under attack from a mocking inner critic who says, "There you go — inadequate again!"

Recently I decided to challenge that voice. "So I'm inadequate," I replied. "Is that grounds for attack? Maybe the problem isn't my insufficiency, but rather my inability to be truly present to myself and to my life!" When looked at from that perspective, my inadequacy could be due to the fact that I've absented myself from what's most precious — The Pearl Without Price, the Crest Jewel in the Crown, or The One Thing Necessary cited by the sages — without which nothing else has meaning.

Some would refer to it as turning back to God. Others advocate listening to the still, small voice that's probably always trying to catch our attention — the voice we seldom hear because we don't have the time or inclination to listen. Yet, from time to time, as we go about our daily activities, we are aware of an echo — a sense that something is missing, that perhaps we are absent to the meaning of our presence on this earth.

There are many metaphors for the insufficiency of our response to life's demands, but in the end it's all about presence. If we could own the sense of inadequacy at the very moment the self-attack appears, it could awaken the question, "What's the one thing I need right now?" Then we might discover what's really going on. Then we could ask, "Am I lost in a corner of myself? Is there a way to access a larger view?"

Day 1
Look at it this way: even you sometimes feel inadequate — or stupid or helpless at this or that moment — haven't you left something out of the equation you so quickly arrived at? Whenever you feel inadequate to a situation today, stop to investigate: is it true? Or are you dealing with two levels here that can only be related through your own recognition that you both are and are not present to your life.

Day 2
As soon as you wake up to the fact that you are both nothing and someone, you stand between two worlds, one above and one below you. At that moment of awareness, you become a conscious link between them. You are both nothing and yourself, and a particle of the universe as life unfolds in and around you. Choose to stand between two worlds whenever you can today.

Day 3
Looked at from a larger perspective, the sense of inadequacy is an essential vibration we all need to tune into more often. Isn't presence often about being present to our absence? Try to listen to the vibration that accompanies your sense of inadequacy. Beyond the judgmental accusation, it is telling you something you need to know. Find out whether the resonance of presence to your life is absent from you, or whether you are perhaps absent from it.

Day 4

With the discoveries of the last few days in mind, "Who am I?" is the operative question today. Surely you are a living, breathing entity linked like the stars to millions of other entities, interdependent with them, both needing and serving them. So when faced with such a scale, is there any room for self-attack or self-denigration? It's unreal and inaccurate even though we engage in it every day. So next time you criticize yourself, remind yourself that you have a place on earth, however miniscule it may be. You are needed, in some way perhaps unknown to you, for this earth's survival.

Day 5

By exploring such questions you will arrive at a big one: "Am I absent to reality?" Raise it this very day. In his book, The Ease of Being, the Hindu teacher Jean Klein points to a feeling of emptiness brought about by a state of self-questioning. He says we hunt in many directions for something to fill our sense of lack, followed by a moment of peace when we get what we thought we wanted. But soon we'll be off again, "like a hunting dog who cannot find the scent," in frantic search for what we think we can't do without. Sound familiar? Although nothing satisfies us for long, he points out, it is through this repetitive lure of wanting that we become more and more attracted to what he calls "the scent of reality."

Let Them Go

At the beginning of this morning's yoga class, the teacher asked us to focus our attention on the multicolored trees outside. "Trees lose their leaves in order to save themselves," she said. That startled me. Why does something so beautiful require such a sacrifice? Then she explained that trees have to let their leaves go so their energy won't be sucked dry. They know when it's time to prepare for winter.

There's a lot to learn from that. I, for one, have trouble letting go of the past. I become stuck in my yesterdays whether I dwell on negative reactions and sorrows, or the high points of days gone by. But when I stop to think about it, life both outside and inside me is in constant movement — from the flow of oxygen-rich blood that nourishes my body to the flow of impressions from each living moment that nourish the soul. I need to let go of the past, just like the trees.

If I were able to let go of the past I could accept a winter of suspended animation so that spring's promise of rebirth could become a reality. But how to allow my own dead and dying leaves to detach themselves and blow away on the winds of change? I stood on the mat in Mountain pose, looking at the trees outside, and asked myself: "What do I need to let go of to save my life?" The first leaf I wanted to give up, red with my own blood, is the tendency to judge others and myself. "Let it go," cried a voice deep inside me. Then I noticed yellow leaves of self-pity and brown ones full of self-justification. Unfortunately, wherever I caught sight of the ego's demands, they were still bright green.

Maybe a first step to letting go would be to try sometimes to hold back the energy I spend on wanting things, along with all those thoughts about yesterday or dreams of tomorrow. That way I could nourish the present moment with today's life-energy. But it's so hard to remember to do that when I'm magnetized by the attraction of past or future.

"Help me do this," I prayed to whatever higher source might be available. "It seems I'm not very good at doing it for myself." Then I remembered that Seeing comes first, long before Doing, long before making changes. So I try to see how and why I hold onto the past. And while it may be a long way home to my Self, as long as I keep the trees in mind, I know I'm already following the right path. What's more, I suspect that somewhere in each of us, in a place we seldom trust, grows a whole forest of evergreens.

When you examine your situation consciously, do you sometimes wonder where all this present suffering comes from? Could the pain spring from a childhood encounter, a demanding parent, or your own personal expectations? What's important is to be present to your life — to be here now. To do that, you must learn to let go of the past and allow those dried up leaves to blow away wherever the wind wants to carry them. They no longer belong to you.

Day 1
The first step to letting go of the past is seeing how hard you hold onto it. Just notice your thoughts and feelings whenever past wounds or successes fill you during the day. Write each of them down. At the end of the day you can take your list and put the individual items into general categories, giving a name or a color to each category. Find your own way to do this, but here are some of mine: "I wasn't understood." "They made me mad." "Wow, that turned out well!" "I wish I hadn't said that." "He has no right!"

Day 2
Now, with your categories in mind, gather more examples of how you hold on and hold back. Are last night's dreams still mesmerizing you? Are you still muttering about the guy who bumped against you in the subway? How did the woman who stopped talking when you came into the ladies' room make you feel? Place any resentments or reactions into your categories, and add new ones if necessary. Begin to recognize how much they interfere with your possibility of living in the present.

Day 3

Seeing *is what's important here — to see how and why you store up resentments or bad feelings about yourself or others in a kind of inner refrigerator. Be alert today to what offends or disappoints you and why. Begin to notice the judgments you make all day long about everything. Do you hold onto certain rules or prejudices without having examined why you believe in them? IF you write them down you can reexamine them later with your best intelligence.*

Day 4

Dig deeper today. Is there one category that stands out, that repeats itself more than others? Or is one of them more hurtful to you? Do you tend to feel angry more often, or victimized? Which do you hold onto longer, resentments of others or bad feelings about yourself? Write all of this down. Then see if you can figure out what triggers any of those feelings. Maybe there's a button others press that never fails to activate your reaction. Once you know that, maybe you can figure out where the button is that deactivates it.

Day 5

One way to find that button is to think back to your childhood days to see if there's a source from which some of these resentments or bad feelings spring. Try that today. No judgments; just observations. What's important is to uncover, at the very moment of the reaction, what in you is holding onto the past and why. Once you are able to discover that, you're more than halfway to letting go.

Pain in the Heart

The other day, when I realized how tense I had become, I asked myself what was going on. Immediately I felt a strong emotional constriction along with aching limbs. In other words, I was in pain without having consciously perceived it. As I began to digest that fact, and receive the information it provided, the intensity eased. I was reminded once again of my tendency to avoid suffering, as well as the need to connect more often to how I feel.

Another morning as I walked to the subway, tired and aching all over, I queried the body: *"Where* are you tired?" Immediately there was a soft blow in my solar plexus and my body let go in relief. Once I accepted to feel the pain in my heart, the rest of me was no longer held hostage in a general vise of tension.

We know that the body carries our emotional pain when we are unable to process it. Then why are we so often unaware of how we really feel? Why focused so intensely on the next problem in the day's agenda that there's no time for the heart to speak, here and now? It seems that only with an effort of attention to the present moment can thought form a bridge to a quieter state, like the inner world we visit in meditation — the world we tend to forget about the rest of the day.

As soon as we shelve our subtle connection with the Self in favor of necessary functioning in the outer world, we become lost in Doing. However, if we were to take time to ask the right questions, the mind could reconnect us with both worlds, inner and outer, simultaneously, which might lead to heartfelt realizations. Questions create that needed link: "Who am I? Why am I here? How do I feel? What is the one thing necessary for me right now?"

Although we too seldom engage in them, such queries have a high function. Like fingers pointing at the moon, they guide the attention to whatever state we have been unknowingly imprisoned in. They awaken another point of view, a new place on which to stand, and from which to accept the suffering we tried to avoid. While we may not get rid of the heart's pain, we begin to own our life. And to work this magic we have only to begin an honest examination of what's going on right now, in spite of the fact that it may hurt to do so.

Like me, you probably spend much of your life collecting aches, pains and emotional reactions. But who is this Self, this some-body who-was-there-all-the-time and lives in another room of your inner mansion? Welcome to the many rooms you may have forgotten about or never known existed in you. Once you become aware of them, you'll find more space to move about. Light and a fresh breeze will stream in through the windows as you open to the greatness that lies within you.

Day 1
Step one: to find out what's really going on, you need to wake up to the vague discomfort of physical pain or emotional constriction. Only then can you register it rather than deny, consciously or unconsciously, that something's wrong. Your body will tell you how rigid you are: tense fingers, clenched jaw, stiffened legs, tight stomach, aching back. And as you pause to acknowledge their existence, hopefully these tensions will begin to release.

Day 2
The second step is to turn toward the pain, rather than away from it. Give up trying to avoid it, or refusing to acknowledge it till you "feel better." As you accept to be in pain, you may discover a reactive, complaining, fearful, angry, or just-plain-tired person within. Pay attention, because she's probably been there for a while. Let your mind open to the sensations and feelings that appear, without holding back.

Day 3
Third, don't argue with them (something we all do so well!). Accept that they are real. You will often have thoughts that insist, "it's too late," or "there's no point worrying about it now," or simply "you've got to grit your teeth and bear it." While you don't have to grit your teeth, bearing it is exactly what's required. As William Blake states in Songs of Innocence and Experience,

92

" . . . we are put on earth a little space,
That we may learn to bear the beams of love."

Day 4
Step Four is possible only when you've successfully negotiated the previous three stages. Catch yourself today at any time you feel you are at the helm of your own ship; then come about, and drop anchor. As you come to a stop, observe the inner winds, the power of the tides, and whether the stars are in line with the course you set yourself earlier. That way, you become a receiver of information, rather than the person who imagines he or she is in control.

Day 5
Today, as you become aware of another presence within you, and listen to the information provided by body, mind and emotions, you can begin to process whatever the pain needs you to know. As Khalil Gibran said, "Your pain is the breaking of the shell that encloses your understanding." Breaking the shell is Step Five, where you begin to listen to your Self.

Great Expectations

When I look forward to something — a vacation, a party, meeting someone new, making a big change in my life, I'm often disappointed. The event, the person, the trip, wasn't what I expected, and has left me feeling cheated. I discovered that as a kid. So from then on I worked hard to convince myself ahead of time that the next special event wouldn't be any fun, in hopes the odds might change. Sometimes the ploy even seemed to work. But it's a pretty convoluted approach to life!

As the Buddha pointed out, our emotions (and therefore often our life's outlook) tend to seesaw back and forth between hankering for something and dejection at not getting what we want. So here's an alternative way to look at our tendency to harbor great expectations. Whenever I expect too much from the future or become too depressed when things didn't pan out, I could think of it as a wake-up call to tell me I've lost my balance. My sense of Self is off-kilter.

"Life," as John Lennon so elegantly said, "is what happens when you're making other plans." Isn't that true for all of us? So when my soul's contentment depends on future successful outcomes or I'm devastated by what life has served up on my plate, I turn my attention to my present life. As soon as my mind focuses on whatever immediate demands I need to meet and what my hands and feet are doing right now, disappointments gradually fade into the background.

The most important reason to avoid great expectations is that they are a source of suffering. We are all heroes of our own romance, but reality intrudes on us all day long. What I expect from life, how I expect others to be, how I want them to react to me, and what I want from them, can all become a source of distress. Even more painful are my exaggerated expectations of myself, and my unsatisfied dreams of personal success.

Let's look at the word *romance*. It has two definitions. The first, as might be expected, is associated with love. But the second gives pause: "a quality or feeling of mystery, excitement, and remoteness from everyday life." Yes, mystery and excitement are exhilarating, but does it make sense to spend the time of our lives remote from our everyday life? That's where each of us has to make a choice. We all know what the Buddha chose.

Jose Ortega y Gasset tells us bluntly: "The most salient characteristic of life is its urgency, 'here and now' without any possible postponement. Life is fired at us point-blank." So disappointment can invade you at any moment. It changes the quality of your feelings about yourself and your life. The solution is, of course, to live in the present moment. That's what the Buddha had in mind.

Day 1
Today, study in more detail what disappoints you and why. How long do such feelings usually last? What do they depend on? Your assignment isn't to change how you feel (a losing proposition since we have little control over our emotional reactions), but to examine your reactions through intelligent reasoning about what's going on right now. Then make a list of some of the expectations and disappointments that have colored your life in the past.

Day 2
To define hankering and dejection as loss of balance offers an alternative to bewailing your fate. When you've lost something, where do you look for it? Surely in the last place you remember seeing it. So when you have feelings of resentment or regret today, go back in your mind to the last time you felt good about yourself, or enjoyed a trip or social event, a walk in the park or even a quiet day at home. Let that memory flood your consciousness as you bring the two states, past and present, together in your mind and heart. Try to stand consciously between them to receive an impression of the complex, sometimes divided being that you are.

Day 3
We react to the blows and sweet winds of life in many ways, but often our reactions are a result of the "rules" we lay down ahead of time: "This should be fun," or "What a drag that will be!" And a frequent under-

tone afterward is: "That ought not to have happened." Notice whether such expressions or attitudes color your outlook as you go through your day. How much do you expect from each event? On what do you base those expectations?

Day 4

Today, experiment with taking a new view of whatever your current situation may be. Like all of us, you are usually forced to accept what comes. But you do have a choice in how you receive life's blows in the world of your body, mind and attention. Once confronted with the inevitable, study the when and why of it to discover whether your disappointment results from inflated expectations.

Day 5

Yesterday's exercise may indicate that, like the rest of us, you tend to make judgments ahead of time, before the event or before meeting with another person. So, just for today, determine to give up this habit of judging everything previous to the actual event. If you are able to make the attempt, you'll begin to see more clearly where your inner hankering and disappointment are coming from. Then, ask yourself, "What do I really want right now?"

Quiet Needs

Have you noticed how some things you really need are quite quiet? So quiet you may not know you need them until you've been without them for too long. They don't gnaw at you like hunger for food or sex, or tickle you like "I want an ice cream" or "Let's go see a good movie." And they are not like the open longing kids have for a bicycle and grownups for a car.

This morning I felt such a need. It came in the form of uneasiness, a sense of absence. Without knowing what it was about, I attempted to stifle it with chores, accusing myself of trying to avoid the work that needed doing. But it was no use. I walked out of the house wondering where I was going. There was stuff to buy and stuff to deliver, but my feet took me to the park (definitely against my conscious intention, since I'd planned to go there later in the day).

As I entered the path, bordered on each side by great trees lush with the spring rains of the last few days, my pace slowed. My heart opened. I realized that here I was, at last, where I was meant to be! As the unease subsided, the natural world reached out to me and I opened to it, filled with gratitude that I had been led, albeit reluctantly, to what I was really looking for. I had been met in my most quiet need.

Such a need often goes unrecognized amidst the demands of daily life. Sometimes I don't even know I'm lonely until I turn away from whatever I was concentrated on and see that Gatsby, my orange fur-ball of a cat, is watching me intently from a few feet away. He meets me where I'm unconsciously desperate to be: in relationship. There he is, waiting to be seen, waiting to be loved and to love in return.

He's not a demanding cat, any more than the park demands my presence. He's just there, waiting till I'm ready to pet him or engage in play. His longing look tells me he needs to be brushed or fed or loved. Maybe there's someone quietly waiting inside me, with equal patience, hoping for my attention.

Needs can be simple. Needs can be quiet. It's we who lose out if we wait too long; if we don't try harder to recognize and respect them, to seek more actively to discover what our real needs are.

Contrary to what we usually believe, you don't have to be physically still to experience a larger impression of yourself. It may be easier when you bring yourself to a complete stop, but Jesus said, "I am a movement and a rest." Your deeper being resides in you wherever you go, whatever you do. Listen for it this week.

Day 1
Spend some of your "down" time today listening to yourself and the world around you. To do this, you may have to give up judging whether you have time for this or whether it's right or wrong to feel the way you feel. The judge is useful for moral issues and to weigh consequences but he gets in the way when what you want is to develop a moment of inner peace. Once he's out of the way, deep listening can dissolve into inner quiet, a state devoutly to be wished but not easily attained amid the conflicting demands and longings of life.

Day 2
The Navaho path is called Walking in Beauty or hozho naasha — *the Blessing Way. What could that mean to you?* Hozho *refers to the natural order. Imagine for a moment that beauty exists within and all around you. Think about how you could walk in beauty today, how you might live in a loving way and in right relationship to your neighbor and to the elements. We all step out of this path too often, but what's important is learning how to find our way back. That's what this book is about.*

Day 3
Take a walk that includes walking away from whatever may be your present problem to solve. Begin to notice your weight on each foot and the rhythmical sway of your hips as one leg and then the other moves forward. Imagine your pelvic plate as a tray on which your upper body sits as your legs take the rest of you for a walk. Listen to the sounds

around you and the voices within you, wondering what you'll hear next. Tune into it.

Day 4

The natural world can be very helpful when you feel a desperate need to refresh yourself. While we often look around rather passively as we walk in park, woods or countryside, as if seeing it through a plate glass window, nature is always teeming with activity. Look around you at the "meanest flower that grows" and the tallest trees. Listen to them. Stand still for a minute among them. Become aware of the active strength and confidence of trees. Let them talk to you. They are truly "here." And you, too, have hidden roots in the earth, just as they do, invisible to the casual eye.

Day 5

From time to time today you might give up "running the show," whatever occupation you are in the middle of. If you're in the office and don't want to seem lazy, go for your coffee break. Take that time to listen to yourself rather than fantasize or solve problems. Or stop what you're doing at your desk at any time, to give your mind a few moments to settle down and away from its busyness. Focus on yourself as a three-dimensional being who lives in several worlds.

What to Give Up?

Do you, too, feel strongly that there's not enough time for every-thing, and that in order to focus on what's important, some things have to be put aside? The question is, how to choose? What to give up? Marion Woodman puts it more dramatically: "What must be sacrificed?" For it is indeed a sacrifice — my attention must be focused in one direction or another.

Often it's the small stuff that must be put aside, the irrelevant stimuli and self-affirmations that distract me from my central aim, since time becomes more precious as I get older. And even more important is the need to separate myself from obsolete inner attitudes that hold me to fixed patterns of thought and action, limiting the growth of my being.

It's not that such stimuli and habits are bad or wrong, or that I must always say no to them, but they distract me from the life I seek to live. When I put them aside, it's in the name of something more important: my wish to live richly in the service of a higher value, and to be present to both worlds as often as possible, not just the one I'm usually stuck in.

In order to know what to sacrifice, I must first learn to make choices. Gurdjieff says, "Only he deserves help from above who can keep alive both the wolf and the sheep given into his care." The wolf, I now see, isn't just the angry, jealous, competitive, crit-ical part of me I've begun to know pretty well. It is also, quite simply, Appetite. So there's work to exercise choice on a quite practical level. At any moment, what do I need most, a TV program or inner quiet? A slim and vibrant body, or the momen-tary yumyum of a macaroon?

It's up to me to study my habits and longings and ask, "What do I value most?" The question resounds on many levels, from the need to turn aside from whatever invades me in the form of over-stimulation and unnecessary pressure, to the need to examine why I eat what I eat. As Jean Anthelme Brillat-Savarin wrote in his *Physiology of Taste, or Meditations on Transcendent Gastronomy*, "Tell me what you eat and I will tell you what you are."

As you get older, you may find that your growing accumulation of things from the past becomes a burden, especially if you have to move to a smaller house or apartment. It may be hard to unburden yourself — fewer 'things' means fewer ties to the past, which can be both good and bad. In any case, if you are faced with such a dilemma, think of aligning yourself with the millennial message of Lao Tsu: "In the pursuit of learning, every day something is acquired. In the pursuit of Tao, every day something is dropped."

Day 1
Today's question may seem obvious, but not necessarily easy to figure out: What do you really want? Only when you have some clarity about what you value can you decide what's worth keeping and what to give up. So take time to ask it of yourself at different moments during the day. Don't expect an immediate response. As you start out, you are looking for a direction to go toward, rather than a target. Were you a Zen archery student, you'd be at the stage of learning to string and lift the bow and arrow without yet taking a shot.

Day 2
Once you have a clearer sense of direction you will be able to move forward, most likely in baby steps. Take time in the morning, before the day gets going under its own steam, to examine what's on your list of activities and entertainments. Select a few less important items that can be put aside, either till tomorrow or forever. Sometimes what you decide to give up will be appropriate, sometimes not, but you'll soon find out. Learning to discriminate is part of the process. Remember, the Zen master looses his arrow with his eyes closed but it finds its way to the center of the target.

Day 3
On the other hand, sometimes it's just not possible to know what to aim for. Today your task is not to prepare ahead of time, but to weigh and choose what to do at each moment, on the fly, by the seat of your pants,

according to the information each moment has to offer. Let the wisdom of instinct and intuition guide you, rather than following yesterday's rulebook.

Day 4
Do you harbor a negative critic who constantly gets in the way of your ability to decide what's really important? In that case, inform him firmly that he is not you. He doesn't know everything about you, and there are times when he is no help at all. Here's a useful prayer: "Let my life no longer be ruled by a black-robed judge who condemns and criticizes everything. I wish to see life as a constantly changing, three-dimensional kaleidoscope of many colors and find ways to adapt to it with the best of my intelligence."

Day 5
Do you wonder why we live in fixed patterns, defending ourselves from what's going on right now? Why do we approach everything as if it can be set in only one way, as if there's only one cause and one solution? Freedom lies in letting go of patterns. Today, look for the patterns that trap you into repetition, and note them down. If you can, wash them right out of your hair and meet life as it comes toward you, attending and responding to the unknown.

Anxiety

We often waken to the unfolding of a new day with a fresh, unfettered mind for just a few moments. Then the memory of things we need to get done, people to see, problems to resolve, floods us with anxiety. Soon the morning becomes oppressive, filled with the knowledge of what we must do and the question, spoken or unspoken, of whether or not we can handle it all. Like a sack full of bricks which we hurry to empty before we're overwhelmed, anxiety weighs us down.

Anxiety can even haunt our dedicated morning meditation like a scarcely heard vibration. Or there may be intense pressure in the chest, the jitters, a sense of nervous insecurity. And even when our efforts at equanimity somewhat quiet the pressure, a rising undercurrent often resurfaces as soon as we go into action — the beginnings of panic because we'll never get it all done, no matter how hard we try. As Joan Borysenko so astutely put it in *Inner Peace for Busy People*, "Your to-do list is immortal. It will live on long after you're dead."

Later in the day we may feel different — more annoyed than panicked — unsatisfied at the day's performance and irritated because this really isn't how we want to spend the hours of our life. Dark shadows of self-accusation gather. "How could I have forgotten such and such? Why couldn't I have done a better job at this or that? Here I am, once again failing to do what HAD to be done or not doing it as well as I thought I should."

By evening, anxiety often lets go its hold. We are exhausted enough to give up feeling as if the world would end if all we needed to accomplish were not done. Does anyone want to live like that? Absolutely not! But what action could we undertake to release anxiety's grip on us, and yet get through all we have to do? One thing's sure: in order to unhook ourselves from habitual emotional states like anxiety and self-doubt, work and dedication are required.

To begin with, let's be clear about the difference between fear and anxiety. An anxious state may convince you that you are afraid, but there's a big difference between them. Fear invades you when you are faced with present bodily harm, confronted by a lion in the street. An immediate surge of adrenalin gives you strength to run and hide. But anxiety is never about present danger. It is always about what might happen in a future that is, in fact, unknown.

Many of us live in perpetual states of anxiety, developed over the years. It's helpful to recognize that anxious states are one-sided — I'm lost in thoughts or emotional reactions which feed on each other to create a rising tide of panic. So if I can become present to the sensation of the state itself — the butterflies or the breathlessness — and focus the mind on the body's sensations, my attention is drawn away from the habitual state of uncertainty I'm stuck in, and toward body consciousness. Each time I become more aware of the sensation of my earthly vehicle, here in real time, anxiety lets go of its viselike grip for a little while.

We are tri-partite beings, and one part sometimes takes over to enslave the other two and steal their energy. Any activity that engages your body and thinking attention together, or creates a new feeling of yourself, will lessen anxiety's chokehold. Each time you move away from its grip, even for a little while, you create space for a new impression of yourself.

Day 1
Your first step to combat frequent anxiety is to notice the undifferentiated undercurrent that haunts you when you feel over-tasked or overwhelmed. Ask yourself, "Is this my habitual state?" Is there a ghost somewhere in your machinery, perhaps a past situation related to your present life, which long ago deflated your sense of self? Turn your attention to other times you've felt anxious, as far back as you can remember. Write them all down and, later in the day, ponder the incidents you recall, even try to relive them in your mind.

Day 2
A habitual state of anxiety usually blossoms out of unprocessed experiences from the past. For example, most of us are worried about how we

look. There's a hidden sense of insecurity from states of self-doubt in childhood, when you weren't seen as the person you felt yourself to be, but judged on how you looked. Notice how often you check yourself out in a mirror today and what thoughts are going through your mind at that very moment. What do you worry about as you look? Nothing wrong with inspecting yourself, but there are clues in the thoughts that it provokes.

Day 3
Today try to recognize where anxiety expresses itself in your body (mostly below the conscious mind). It will attack different places in different people: butterflies in the pit of the stomach, hyperventilation, a clenched jaw, an aching head, or fists balled up as if ready to strike someone. Try to become sensitive and alert to whatever part of your body expresses unnecessary tension. It may be a signal that you are anxious even though the reason is under your radar. Once physical symptoms betray the vibration of an anxious state, you've been informed of what you need to know. The next step is up to you. Ask yourself, what is really going on here? Write down your immediate thoughts.

Day 4
Maybe your office is piled with papers that need your attention. Or your heart is filled with memories that haunt you because they haven't yet been properly digested. While the papers need work and the memories need reflection, if they berate or grieve you all the time, you are, in effect, their prisoner. In that case, an invitation to deeper body consciousness could help you refocus. Perhaps a long brisk walk would do it, or a swim, or some other form of physical exercise could lead your heart, mind and body into a better balance.

Day 5
Today, on the other hand, you could engage with whatever you are anxious about. Talk to it. Ask it why it pursues you, what it wants from you, why it won't let you go. Then try to write down any comments that appear in your head, without making judgments. Every time I've done this, I've always learned something new, although the language it's phrased in may be strange, crude and unpleasant. You can also express your grief or consternation using paint and paper, or molding clay in your hands, or dancing the anxiety away. Let your paints, hands or body do whatever they want. Your job is simply to observe what's expressing itself through you.

The Rejected Cornerstone

Until recently, the architects of my life have been busy building, although I always called it "seeking." The search was not for the almighty dollar, or even a roof overhead. My ambition was spiritual: to perfect myself as a human being.

As a child I always demanded the "true truth," according to my mother. Naive and determined, I hunted it down wherever it seemed hidden and often exposed it, gratis. Nobody thanked me for that! In my teens, I sought the handsome prince who would carry me off to happily-ever-after land — a ten-year manhunt that ended in a wedding, and led to a family that means the world to me. My work as a writer, journalist and teacher trained me further in hunting for answers.

Now, at the other end of a life — well, not the end exactly, hopefully with a few years still to go — all this has changed. Instead of pushing, discovering, seeking perfection, looking for a sense of success in new achievements, I began to wonder what it's all been for. Who were these builders who worked so hard to make me what I am — or what I seem to be? And did they ever throw out the baby with the bathwater?

No doubt these construction engineers were necessary for my growth, helpful on a certain level, and not to be despised. But now it's time for them to retire, to take their place as servants, not master builders. Maybe they thought they knew what they were doing, but there's a lot they and I didn't understand as I hurried through my life. For example, I often disparaged certain aspects of myself as childish, inferior, naive, caring too much, hesitant, messy, not very smart.

Today I celebrate these rejected aspects of myself as I watch them bloom into new depths of feeling. In any case, the architects of my perfect truth, my perfect marriage and my perfect self long ago abandoned the cornerstone of the person I would now like to be. Any plans for my perfection have crumbled into the same earth we are all headed for some day. Now I stand on a new foundation, uncertain, unknowing, wondering, yet full of joy. This is me. All of me. Imperfect me. Juicy me! I resonate with the Buddha's cry, after his long night of temptations: "Thou art seen, O Builder. Never again wilt thou build house for me!"

Are you looking to rebuild your life on a solid foundation with a cornerstone set in reality? If so, here are a few steps you might want to adopt in order to make a fresh start to each day.

Step 1
Maybe you woke up this morning feeling good. But if you're tired or depressed, or somehow off-kilter, the day may have to be built from scratch. In that case, you will have to forklift yourself out of the bed you lie in, resisting what's in store. To do this, imagine that a small crane takes hold of your legs and swivels you around as your back pops up to a sitting position, feet on the floor. Go with it! At that new vantage point, you can see the world from the vertical, human dimension. Now call on the mind, your best tool for organizing movement, to help you rise and stagger down the hall to do whatever helps you step into your day.

Step 2
Next, you might begin to build a morning habit of a few stretching exercises, followed by quiet meditation. It's something I've been doing for many years, and I recommend it because, whether I feel like it or not, it's helpful to have a routine that gets me moving, even before morning coffee. What's more, stretching will wake up parts of you that are still half asleep and release nighttime aches and pains as your musculature warms up.

Step 3
Meditation may be your ticket to the present moment. Sit cross-legged on the floor, kneel on a Japanese sitting stool, or find a straight-backed chair. When you are seated on a solid base, your spine will be upright, like a column of light that connects above and below, heaven and earth, your head and your butt. Now tune in step by step to what's going on in every part of your body/mind/heart. If you give it time, help often comes. Even if you're tired, a new energy may gradually fill you, along

with the sensation of you, here in your body, open to the unknown, to whatever's going on in your life. The awakening sense of your body's form may bring a new feeling to the heart. Happy or sad, you've found a more solid foundation for your day.

Step 4
Nevertheless, some serious construction work may still be needed, especially when physical, mental or emotional discomfort hangs on as it sometimes does. Reading something inspirational at breakfast could stir your interest or enlarge your thought, giving further direction to your day. If you've no book in mind, check out the bibliography offered at the end of this book.

Step 5
Now it's time to make a plan. One thing I've learned is that no matter how low or uncertain I may feel, at some point I'll feel better if I get a few things done. What can you do today that will feed body and soul, and also enhance your checkbook? If even only a small a part of your equipment begins to go into action, more of you will soon be tempted to join the dance of life. Your *life.*

Up the Down Ladder

Sometimes we're "up;" sometimes we're "down." While we may prefer the former, we also know that whatever goes up will come down. That means there's no way to avoid the downs by working harder to stay up. We can't even prolong the one and shorten the other just by wishing to do so. But how about climbing up more often when we've been down? Surely that's within the range of our all too fragile human possibility.

P. D. Ouspensky says that we're always trying to alter the inevitable (as in wishing two and two didn't add up to four). But he adds that while there isn't much we can change just by wishing, it's always in our power to develop a new attitude. I bet the Dalai Lama would agree with that. Once, as he walked out of an event, surrounded by journalists, he was asked whether he was different from ordinary people. He replied that indeed he wasn't. The only difference was that every morning when he got up, he "adjusted" his attitude.

There are times when all of us need to adjust our attitude, but perhaps we don't take the suggestion seriously enough. We don't see that our inner life, our soul's balance, depends on unburdening ourselves as quickly as possible of the reactions that drive us down into negative space. Otherwise, like festering wounds, such emotions can erode the delicate fabric of our feeling life. And if we hang onto them too long they can even become semi-permanent.

Not only do we hold onto negative reactions, we also take on other people's moods as if they were our own. You say something angry to me. Although I'd been feeling fine a minute ago, I react with annoyance and reply in kind. Or you tell me something sad, and that makes me sad too. The positive aspect to this tendency is that your good mood can elevate mine, which illustrates our heartfelt human ability to empathize with another's situation.

In any case, we long for peace, to breathe fresh air untainted by negative emotional burdens. But, hey, then why are we so easily trapped into reacting to someone else's hostility? Why is another person's dark mood so magnetic that yours or mine is changed by it? If we could realize how powerfully our moods affect others, we might make more of an effort to transform them. But just push the wrong button and our reactive machinery will go into high gear.

Speaking of fresh air, we city dwellers take our children and sometimes ourselves for walks in the park and get out into the country whenever we can. You probably open your windows every day to let the stale air out and the fresh breeze in. How deeply you breathe, and with what enjoyment! Why not bring the same dedication to refreshing your emotional inspirations and expirations? That's the subject for this week.

Day 1

How can you adjust your attitude? One way is to stop the flow before it gets fully under way and compromises all of your being. Try it today. But, for this, you need to prepare yourself in advance, to convince yourself that it's more important to be present than to let loose with your reactions. Then, as soon as you notice rage building up or self-pity flooding in, you can take action. Reason with yourself. Bring your arguments against it to bear with all the force and finesse you'd use to deal with a 9-year-old having a tantrum. Once that negative reaction is in full swing, it will be really hard to put a stopper on the explosion, so remind yourself, early on, that it comes at a high price, payable in your own energy.

Day 2

Today, help yourself conquer any present mood by bringing scale to the situation. Invite a very different impression to fill your inner landscape. For example, visualize yourself outside on a starry night, under millions of visible worlds. Or recall the majesty of the view when you stood at the top of a high mountain range, with peak upon peak revealed below you. Or imagine yourself on a boat, caught in the tremendous power of a storm at sea. (Where did the expression "tempest in a teapot" come from?)

Day 3

Another way to climb up the down ladder is to remind yourself of the aftereffects of losing your cool in the past. Whatever you're sorry you said or did, revisit the regret. When something makes your gorge rise or your confidence wilt today, ask yourself how you would rate this complaint on a larger scale. Does whatever you're upset about really matter in the larger scheme of things? And at the moment a negative emotion initiates, question whether you really want to use up all your jet fuel in one blast. Ask yourself out loud, "Is this how I want to spend my precious energy today?

Day 4

An alternative method is to let go your hold on whatever is dragging you down by visualizing an up. We tend to cling to emotional reactions. For example, outrage, irritation, resentment, jealousy and self-pity are all downers. Look at it from another perspective. If, while you were swimming, your foot got snagged in a heavy object that dragged you under water, you'd work pretty hard and fast to get free because your life depends on it. Well, believe it or not, the quality of your inner life depends on not being dragged down by every passing mood!

Day 5

No less effective is what probably keeps the Dalai Lama buoyed up by all his positive energy: meditation. If you begin every day with a time of quiet, allowing stillness to grow in both body and mind as you open to the largely unknown world of your inner being, you will at first create, then deepen an alternative path for your energy. It invites you to return more often to the depths of your being during the day. Again, it's a question of scale. You are so much more than rancorous thoughts or emotional storms. There's a world of finer feelings in you at a deeper level. Any time you connect with it, you're home free.

Making No Demand

I was sitting in the park the other day, one of those nice, warm April days that take us by surprise. Newly sprouted daffodils glinted everywhere, and the forsythia seemed to shine with its own sunlight. Although I'd brought along some editing to do and an "important" to-do list to mull over, I asked myself, "What would happen if I stopped my busyness and made no demand on myself at all? What will come if I give it all up and sit here and wait for a few minutes?"

So I sat and waited. I listened to noises one doesn't usually hear, and admired the haze of green on the trees that would shortly become abundant growth. And I was changed.

Birdsong became music, for one thing — a variety of notes and rhythms, trills and single sounds, and, behind them the slight buzz of insects barely daring to come forth into the spring. My breathing deepened, for another.

At first I thought maybe I was just more aware of it. But, no, the change was larger than that. I was entering into a new relationship with myself. No longer was the mind ordering the physical equipment around. Instead of the outer-directed person I'd been a few minutes ago, I had become a living, breathing being, sitting here at rest.

Which makes me ask, why do I use myself the way I mostly do, as if this body is only there to get stuff done, never calculating the quality of the service? The fact is, my body almost always tries hard to do whatever I ask of it. It makes an honest effort to serve my intention. But my head brain often forgets it is also a servant, and roams around following its fancy, seldom taking the body's needs and desires into account.

As I sit and muse on these things amid the smells of park and city, the impression deepens. Here I am, in this beautiful place, mysteriously alive in the five-foot, seven-inch container that I am. And words spring forth: "Lord, let me grow and prosper in Your service; mind, body and whatever else I am!"

Thus I become aware, sitting on a park bench, how "making no demand" melts into prayer.

How are you using yourself today? That's the question F. M. Alexander asked his students. He wanted them to experience the disconnect between their neuromuscular being, their reactive psyche and the often autocratic head brain that thinks it runs the show.

Day 1
Investigate which of them is running your show at different times during the day. What's really important to you at this or that moment? And do you give time to release the tensions that gather as you forge ahead through your day? What might your body require or deserve?

Day 2
It's good to put away your to-do list from time to time and listen to the noises of the world. Do this several times today for a few minutes. You will discover many sounds we seldom hear. Are the ones you notice human, animal, mechanical, or expressions of nature? All these worlds reach out to us in different ways. Which world do you mostly live in?

Day 3
Everything has color, sometimes bright, sometimes muted. While there are thousands of shades to each color, we usually only see a few because we seldom look long enough at what we see. Look around often today, and count how many colors you see. The stores on every street, the clothes people wear, the cars they drive, are all full of color, as is the world of nature around you. Let colors flood your awareness, and stay with each of them long enough to note its shade or tint.

Day 4
Today, bring your focus to your own breathing. Your breath provides you with the rhythm of your life. It is essential to your survival, yet how often are you aware of it? Check on the rhythm of your breathing every

few hours and see how it changes as your moods change. For example, notice it when you feel hurried or tired. From time to time, stop whatever you are doing and notice how your breathing alters again, slower and deeper as you pay closer attention to it. Sense how much of your body moves as you breathe — your chest, belly, back, and shoulders all ride on the breathing.

Day 5
There's another essential rhythm on which your life depends — your heartbeat. You can put your hand on your left chest to see if you can perceive the beating heart directly, but that's difficult. Stop for a few minutes now and then today to appreciate it by putting your right fingertips on the left side of your left wrist to feel your pulse. That's your life beating away! Can you connect this pulse to what in your life is heartfelt — what you really care about?

Variety

They say variety is the spice of life, and it may be true. Life today seems to be grounded in the need for variety — we want to be entertained, interested, engaged. But could it be hazardous to our health to live with so much stimulation? Yes, it makes life interesting, but does it feed the Being?

There is in me a small central core — tiny, perhaps, but truly me. It is simple, slow, quiet, gentle and easily disturbed. My attention is attracted from all sides by duties, thoughts and sensations, as well as a taste for variety, which can confuse and sometimes even overwhelm me. How many times have I ceased to exist as "me" under the barrage of distractions, attractions and demands for my attention! Could I live more simply? How to orient myself more often within the bandwidth of this small, simple, sacred space of "me?"

I often compare the continuing presence of distraction with the Peruvian *montaña*, where I lived for a few years. Jungle as well as mountain, it teems with all kinds of life, just as, inside and outside my brain, all kinds of disturbances crawl, creep, fly and stalk, endlessly interrupting my attempts at inner quiet.

Even when I try to meditate, distraction comes in many forms — mostly thoughts about things I ought or want to do. Problems to be solved pop into my mind, and idle thoughts surface to interrupt the quieting down of the organism. At that point I'm sometimes reminded of King Henry II's complaint when he ordered his archbishop, Thomas Becket, killed. Then I mutter to myself, " . . . will no one rid me of these meddlesome thoughts?"

But no one will. No help will come if I make no effort to choose where to put my attention, if I remain passive to the stimulus of variety. Like arrows shooting at me from everywhere, distractions come to fill this small, quiet, sensitive space in me that's unable to withstand so much diversion. It's up to me to take some action, to introduce some limitation. So from time to time I turn off the tube, walk away from the World Wide Web, ignore the telephone for a blessed few minutes, and return again to this precious Self that often gets lost in the confusion.

We often forget our deep need for quiet as we go through our day of achieving, solving, hesitating, and wondering if we've done all we should. Yet how refreshing it would be to access a change of state, right in the middle of that busyness! What if you could stop to listen for that quiet space over coffee, in the bathroom, at the desk — by turning your attention away from your paperwork or your digital world?

Day 1
Our daily life is mostly ruled by automatic responses to stimuli, reactions that leave no room for conscious awareness. Notice and make a list of the stimuli that are fired at you this morning. Some will be disorienting, distracting you from your intentions, but some could be useful, even centering. Stimulus is good when it wakens us, not so good when it simply eats up our energy or puts us to sleep. What's certain is that, without conscious awareness, our habitual patterns will rule our choices.

Day 2
As your day gets under way, make a list of all the things you ought or want to do. Then take away a third of it and leave it for tomorrow. That way you will have prepared a little breathing space for yourself. Maybe you'll take the extra time to listen to the world, or to meditate, or perhaps simply to engage in doing each item that's left on your list more thoughtfully and carefully, with more of your presence.

Day 3
What does the word Presence mean to you? Find a few synonyms. How could you be more present to your life today? Write down a few ideas this morning, and experiment with returning to yourself at different moments of the day. Note down what happened then. In the evening you can look at the notes you've made. Did the word presence mean the same thing each time you sought it or experienced it, or was it many-faceted, like a jewel?

Day 4

See if you can bring more of this presence into today's encounters with other people. This is harder. As you interact with them this morning, notice whether you tend to get caught in trying to please them or secretly criticizing them. Don't judge yourself — learn about yourself. Figure out what matters most to you while you are with them. Then, in the afternoon, imagine that each encounter with another person is like two separate worlds that approach each other. What do you want from their world? What do you think they want from yours? Will the two worlds collide, or interact, or enhance each other's atmosphere? It's often up to you.

Day 5

Open more frequently to your inner world today. From time to time, as demands and distractions flood your space, close your eyes and imagine just for a moment that there's another way of functioning that includes more of you, your needs, and even your desires. What do you notice? What do you hear? Perhaps your own heart beating and your own soul calling you home.

Something's Missing
(Apathy)

I was sitting on a bench near the entrance to the park, feeling lethargic and despondent — no energy to get up and walk further. It was noon of a beautiful day, but neither the warm air that caressed me nor the exuberant trees that offered their tenderness could change my mood. Something was missing . . .

"Where has all my vitality gone?" I sighed, discouraged. "Have I fallen into a slough of despond? Shouldn't I be pushing myself to accomplish more?" Then an inner voice replied: "I'm tired of living under so much pressure to get things done!"

Suddenly I realized that's what was missing — the pressure I usually feel that propels me forward through each day. Surprised, I decided to stay with this uncomfortable feeling rather than rush into activity, as I so often do to help myself feel better. "I hear you," I said. "I'll accept to feel the way I feel and go along with this apathy for a little while to see where it leads."

At that moment of acceptance, the dam broke and the tears began. A friend is seriously ill with cancer; relationships are difficult. But I've been caught up in the obligation not to "fall apart" as long as others need me. Now, here, surrounded by nature, at last it became possible to feel what was behind the wall of apathy. As my buried emotions spurted into consciousness like water from a fountain, the sense of heaviness disappeared.

When it was time to go back into the demanding world I had left behind, I followed along the path toward the exit as if walking down a cathedral aisle. At every step I was refreshed by the great trees whose boughs arched overhead — the same trees that, moments earlier, had seemed so mute. Flowers beckoned and butterflies danced in front of me. I realized the world was whole again, and so was I.

When you are overcome by apathy or any other emotion, start by accepting how you feel. We don't have the power to change our emotional states by wishing to, so if you are tired or bored or discouraged or depressed, the first step is to register whether or not, on the surface, you are ignoring or denying it. Before you can attempt to leaven an emotional state, it's necessary to recognize at a deeper level that something's wrong and consciously commit to understanding it better.

Day 1

Today try to see how lethargy, apathy and depression can cover up what's really going on. A change of state will depend on your ability to see more deeply into this very moment. As you become more alert to your moods, notice and write down any surface attitudes or explanations that appear, which may range from "nothing can faze me," to "stop the world, I want to get off!" Ask yourself, "What's really going on behind the smokescreen?" Or you could put it differently: what's the emotion behind the refusal to feel?

Day 2

When we feel discomfort it's often our habit to deaden feeling so as not to accept that we are in pain. As you listen more closely to your inner states, you may discover some quiet voices that can tell you more about why you feel the way you do and what's needed next. Write down any advice you get, and try to act on it today. Does life seem meaningless? That's a major challenge! But sometimes there's a simple complaint — like the other day, when I heard a far-off inner cry, "I just want to sit down!" which told me I'd been on my feet for much too long.

Day 3

You don't want apathy to become a habitual emotional undertone over time, like anxiety. So convince yourself that apathy usually conceals emotions you don't want to feel. Today see if you can trigger the emotion behind it. Put on some music that means a lot to you and sing or weep along with it, from your heart. Dance to it. Allow your emotional states to occupy more space in you. Invite yourself to feel what you really feel, even if it hurts.

Day 4
Here's another approach to states of apathy: dedicate yourself to some challenging practical task that demands all your concentration, both physical and mental. You will create a more balanced relationship between head, heart and body if you follow a difficult recipe, play a musical instrument, build a model airplane, or volunteer for a variety of services in your community. When feeling low, you may be lifted by helping others and engaging in making a difference in the world you live in. Alternatively, if you are faced with an assignment you urgently need to finish for your job, attend to it with the whole of yourself.

Day 5
You can also deal with apathy through activating what neuroscientist Daniel Siegel calls Mindsight: our human capacity to perceive ourselves and others with a degree of separation. It helps us understand our reactive states with more clarity as it integrates the brain, and enhances our relationships. Neuroscience throws a lot of light on what has been so long in the dark: the brain and its relationship to mind and body. Siegel calls it "the embodied brain." On his website, www.drdansiegel.com, he invites us to experiment with his Wheel of Awareness meditation. Try it for yourself next time you feel apathy settling in.

The Great Wave

A few years ago I traveled to Costa Rica with my best friend, who was also approaching her 80th year. It was a voyage into the unknown, perhaps our last great adventure before we settled into a more permanent home life. We arrived at our hostel in late afternoon, after a grueling cross-country ride in a jeep, and went for a dip in the early evening surf on a huge and glorious beach. No one could really swim there because the waves were enormous — it was a surfer's paradise!

That first night I dreamed that a gigantic wave came toward me. On the coast of Peru I'd learned to calculate when to dive through a big roller so as not to be thrown and dragged in the sand. But as this wall of water towered above me, I realized I could neither outrun it nor "handle" it in the many ways I'd been able to deal with just about everything in my eventful life. Unable to gauge when to dive through to the other side, I felt completely helpless. I would have to depend on some unknown intelligence to choose the right moment. As I prepared to dive and almost certainly to die, I gave up knowing what to do and offered myself to the unknown.

Was this dream about the end of my life? Was it telling me how to prepare for whatever future exists after death? If you are, like me, in your sunset years, you may put off thinking about the end of life as long as possible. In youth and the fullness of maturity most of us feel it doesn't apply — only to the elderly. The religious console themselves with thoughts of an afterlife. Jung believes the psyche doesn't die, so, from his point of view, there's no reason for the eternal part of us to fear death. However, the ego, mine and yours, is deeply afraid, because it has no future.

Those who have experienced a serious illness, a near-death encounter, or cared for aged parents may be better prepared to face the reality of life's end. But accepting our own mortality isn't a one-time event. Rather, it's a process that may take years. As our sense of security wanes and more moments of sudden fatigue appear, along with an over-reaction to loud noises and a faltering balance, we are forced to come to terms with it.

But what to do, since the ravages of time are inexorable? While we can and should continue to exercise body and brain every day, the future will inevitably contain even more radical experiences. So it's up to each of us to learn from these intimations of mortality. Let us live more fully the time that is ours, in the life that has been given us, whatever its limitations.

Even in the middle of an abundant life it's useful to think about preparing for death. The fact is that something dies at every moment, and something new is born, so you are more familiar with loss than you may think. In any case, whether you are young or old, openness to the great unknown that is called death will teach you more about life, which is, after all, equally mysterious and just as unknown.

Day 1

One major aspect of such preparation would be learning to accept change — a change in your abilities, your status, even perhaps your capacity to remain independent. Those of us who have lost our worldly power, no longer in command of armies or corporations, or even the little world of family and friends, continue to have an important place in society. Our talent lies in an ability to see through the veils of inaccuracy, fakery and downright lying to the truth of any situation, and tell it like we see it. So take a positive attitude to any changing circumstances today, and practice truth-telling whenever you can.

Day 2

As the years move on, you may find more inner noise overloading your head brain. Songs, phrases, words pop up uninvited, or repetitions of old ideas and judgments may be on the increase at the same time that outer noises become more annoying or more difficult to parse. But behind such new difficulties sits a solid mass of life experience, perhaps a whole library of lived knowledge. You have learned many things, known many people, discovered many truths. So who is this person you are now? Where did he or she come from? There is no such thing as an ordinary life, so in what ways has yours been extraordinary? As you review your life, write down some of the adventures and discoveries that have forged you into the person you are today.

Day 3

It's also time to give space to the existence of a larger world than was dreamt of in your earlier philosophy. It's natural that with every momentary glitch comes an inner gasp of fear. Am I losing mind and memory? Or the use of my legs? While you may feel relatively young and comfortable sitting in an easy chair, how do you feel as soon as you stand up? What's the difference? Whether or not you discover that some of your powers are waning, the important question to engage with today is: what part of you always remains who you are? Write about that today.

Day 4

Seek inner quiet more often. While not to know the future is frightening, even those who are active in the midst of a busy life profit from a habit of daily reflection. Any contact with a quiet place of psychic and spiritual rest offers relief from stress and fear. At such times, acceptance of whatever may come is more possible. Begin to build a connection with the taproot of your Self to refresh you every day. Start today.

Day 5

Take heart if you are getting older. You may face an uncertain future — we all do! — but you are not alone. Many share your new condition and may have discovered a variety of solutions to your specific personal difficulties. If you are less active, you have time to study more. Books abound, universities offer courses, clubs and senior centers offer assistance to adjusting to your new normal. To investigate further, take a look at Gene Cohen's The Creative Age: Awakening Human Potential in the Second Half of Life. *Or Stephen Levine's* Who Dies? *in which he invites us to "cultivate a deeper way of knowing . . . by learning to listen . . . with a delicate balance of a quiet meditative mind and an open loving heart."*

A Clearing in the Woods

Dante reminded us that we might wake up one day in a dark wood, perhaps having been asleep for a long time. Suppose you were to wake up hungry and confused, surrounded by trees and bushes, with no idea how you got there. "Wow!" might be your first thought. "How do I get out of here?" But before panic sends you storming into the undergrowth, perhaps it would be wise to sit down for a moment and acknowledge that you are indeed lost in the woods. Somehow you're stuck in an alien world with no idea how you got here, or what put you to sleep in the first place, days or perhaps decades ago.

At this point it might be a good idea to take a careful look at these particular trees and bushes so that, when you begin to hunt for a way out of your dilemma, you don't go in a circle and end up right back where you started! Tell yourself firmly, "I am lost." Then take stock of what "here" looks like.

What comes next? You could forage through your backpack for a compass. Oops! Maybe you forgot to bring one because you thought you knew where you were going! But if you're lucky (and smart) you'll discover that a compass was built into you at birth. Not many choices where to look for it, and since you will have already checked your clothes and backpack and found nothing useful, it's got to be in the body.

In fact, everything that's really yours on this uncertain terrestrial adventure is in the body, including the head brain that got you where you are today. What's more, you may have been mistreating your earthly vehicle, allowing it to become over-weight or heartsick. Maybe it suffers from one or another disease. Maybe it just feels stressed, unattended and miserable.

Right now, before you start trekking further into the unknown to find a way out, step forthrightly into the present situation and begin to attend to any illness or imbalance in your system. Invite a dialogue between your mind and your body. Perhaps best to start with: "Dear body of mine," (it responds to affection and, remember, it's your only vehicle out of these woods), "what do you need that I've been denying you?"

Listen attentively to any responses, because they may come in a language you never bothered to learn. Think of it as a guessing game. "Could my body's needs be as simple as appropriate foods, loving exercise and a bit of warmth and sunshine?" However, it is likely to be more complicated since you're not just a body. In any case, further studies might lead you to other kinds of food as well as light from another sun.

Here's some good news for those of us lost in the woods. Nobel Laureate Ilya Prigogine, a pioneer in self-organizing systems, tells us that "Small islands of coherence in a sea of chaos have the capacity to shift an entire system to a higher order — in fact nothing else ever does." And she adds more encouragement: "We grow in direct proportion to the amount of chaos we can sustain and dissipate." How much chaos can you sustain?

Day 1
For today, put mind and body to work together in the simplest activities of self-preservation. For example, if you were lost in the woods, you would cut some branches to make a bed, find kindling for a fire to warm yourself, and cook whatever food you can discover. Think about what kind of a bed, sofa or chair would be best for you when at rest from your working day. Very soft might too soft, but very hard would be too unpleasant for your body-being, so look for furniture that's appropriate for your own nature and needs.

Day 2
Next, you'll need to study what to eat. If you were lost in a dark wood you'd look for whichever roots and plants offer the best nourishment, but you'd need to study up, so as not to eat a toadstool instead of a mushroom! Or, speaking practically, you could find an alternative medicine nutritionist to consult on your body/mind needs, for improved inner and outer balance.

Day 3

How to get out of here? Scrounge around in whatever you have with you in this place where you're stuck. Maybe you'll uncover a map you missed the first time around. Or there are many books that might suggest paths out of the dark corners into which you've unwittingly stumbled — some of them listed at the end of this book. But don't forget about the secret source of knowledge hidden within you — an inner guide who knows how to help you if you can learn to listen, and follow the advice.

Day 4

Gradually, as you act to change the quality of your situation, a miracle may bloom right where you're stuck. (Gurdjieff defines miracles as laws from another level acting on our level.) You may discover that this place in which you've found yourself isn't so bad after all. Once you've cut down some of the underbrush, found a stream for water and worked at bedding and feeding yourself, it may begin to look more like a clearing in the woods — a place where you can rest, meditate, and study for your next move. Gurdjieff insists that wherever we find ourselves when we wake up to being lost is the very best place to begin inner work.

Day 5

If you still need more help to figure a way out, put your mind, heart and body to the task of Replay. It will help you remember the way you came in. Looking back, perhaps you can trace your path through the needs, ideals and ambitions that have led you to this very place — propelled by success or failure or by burying yourself too deep in work and life obligations. You may discover that the way in is also the way out, as T. S. Eliot suggested.

Replay

There are times when the past is present to us. It comes alive as our eyes focus on the photo album or the pressed flowers, and the joy and pain of remembering radiates from our hearts. Some of us settle into nostalgia. Others grow brisk and wish to eradicate any hesitant look toward the past in present activity. That's often considered a "healthy attitude" and, until recently, it was mine. I moved away as quickly as possible from what had been, too busy to think about it or tie up loose ends. However, a more serious study of the practice of presence brought me to a new point of view.

Every moment that's clearly lived is timeless. It's always there. Even when we forget, the memory isn't gone but latent, like a photo we put away until the next time we open the album. It appears as a flashback when I take time to recall it. So to link myself, here and now, with a past from which I imagine I've "moved on," can hold deep significance for inner growth.

That thought helps me to better understand my relationship to those I love after they're gone. For example, my mother isn't lost to me so long as she occupies a place in my heart. Perhaps no new facet of our relationship can develop, but I don't even know that for sure. And there are a multitude of encounters between us that haven't been sufficiently digested. It's the same with memories of my husband. Although he's dead, there are many knots that still tie us together, created by our life in common. I'd like to untie some of the harsher ones, but when I think of the many gentle moments of communion, passed over so quickly in the hurly burly of our lives with three growing children, a familiar warmth touches my heart. If I take the time to remember them, I can almost feel the touch of his hand.

Although some impressions from past years may seem quite tangled together, there are many separate threads still to be discovered, woven into our life-tapestry. If we take the time to allow each of them briefly to touch heart and mind, the past that has molded and shaped our lives comes alive again to take its place as part of our present and future life. As William Faulkner wrote in *Requiem for a Nun*, "*The past* is never *dead*. It's not *even past*." So it's worth asking ourselves, "what was going on there that didn't catch my attention the first time around?"

Past memories are like snapshots in a photo album or, better yet, a film that can be played again to help us see more clearly what was going on. The corners and edges of the film will show us what we missed the first time, and even the background may carry important information. Replay gives us the opportunity to catch those moments when we were helplessly caught up in roles we never quite knew how to carry out. New understanding visits us as we pay attention to the good times and bad ones with long departed friends and family. Let's move on, yes, but don't forget to look back as well.

If you wonder, "Why replay? What's past is past. Why bring it alive?" the answer is that any past that is truly gone is already eliminated. But much of it is still present, carried in our minds, our bodies and our emotions. So the exercise of replay can help free us of hidden complexes, resentments, even body aches and pains we've carried for a long time. I was plagued by an aching right leg for a year until a therapist asked me "Whom do you want to kick?" Once I found the answer to that, the ache eased up and finally went away.

Day 1

You might experiment with that today. Study any of your chronic aches, pains or illnesses, to see if you can connect them with any person or incident in your past. If you can uncover the anger or grief that has remained part of you, hidden in your body, you can receive its message, then let it go. A fully experienced emotion doesn't prey on us like those we've refused to process. Some painful places may be obvious — the site of an injury — but what story do they tell that you need to revisit or acknowledge?

Day 2
To study a moment on film in some depth you must slow the projection down. Slowing down is also a key factor in living well and deeply. Today, experiment from time to time with slowing your pace. Choose to enjoy a few particular moments with increased relish, either with a friend or alone. By slowing down, you can live each moment more fully because you are more present to yourself and to the world.

Day 3
Reconnect with past friends and family. It is one of the most useful ways to study the positive influences and emotional burdens that were gifted you by your past life. Close your eyes and try to recall a few memorable situations you were in. Then telephone or email a friend or family member who was present at that incident and ask them what they remember of it. Their memory might be quite different. You could also try to paint a picture of the scene. Let pen or brush lead you into replay. Or put on music, and dance the parts different people played in some watershed event from your past.

Day 4
One certain factor in replay is that it causes deep emotions to well up from the depths of our being. That may be as difficult for you as it was for me. So choose wisely what events you want to replay and what people you want to re-visit in your mind. It's a useful exercise if your aim is to know yourself better as you connect with those you love and visit places where you were happy or sad, strong or vulnerable. I lived in a country house in Connecticut from age five to eight that I still associate with "home." Where was home for you? Pay it a mind's-eye visit several times today. You may find that each time you do, you remember more about it and yourself.

Day 5
As children we were present in a way we seldom are as adults, so it's inevitable that we were hurt. But whatever wounds we avoid thinking about could perhaps begin to heal through replay. As a child you didn't have the life experience to understand why you were denied or even brutalized. But today you can revisit those moments because you're a grown-up. It takes courage to return to those events in your mind, so any pain or denial you may feel deserves your respect. And if you choose to replay a painful situation, stay connected with both worlds, past and present. Try to relate to both of them more completely — the child hand

in hand with the adult you are today. What was your part in the event? What motivated other people who made you suffer? Perhaps if you can figure that out, you can even begin to forgive them.

How to Be?

These days, when I bother to look at what's going on inside me, I notice two very different modes of being-in-the-world. One of them, always at the ready when I'm in the company of others, I've dubbed How'm-I-Doin'?

Based on what Gurdjieff called "inner considering," it is an exaggerated concern for what other people think of you as well as the hope that what they see will impress them. Or, on the other hand, you may feel resentment when they don't treat you as you think you "deserve."

While I've enjoyed the momentary excitement of booktalks, recently I got into trouble. I'd spent four days reading *The Practice of Presence* for a down-loadable audio in a beautiful house by a river. It was both strange and exciting to read my whole book at a rather fast pace into a mike. Perhaps, while there, I ate something I shouldn't. In any case, when I got home, my delicate digestive system faltered, forcing me to cancel a 4-day teaching seminar. I recalled Marion Woodman's words to me a few years back: "When we least expect it, we get thrown off our horse."

When I'm thrown off my horse, whether by physical symptoms or emotional anguish, I'm pushed back into the seemingly small space of myself. Why is that a good thing? Because it wakes me up! My forward impetus comes to a stop and, perhaps disoriented, I fall back on what I am and what I know. Then I regroup myself around the only sensible path (admittedly not as well traveled as the other). I call it the Here-I-Am mode of being. Reoriented by shock, accident, illness or any other difficulty, I return to my own reality.

As I get older, the wish to live more often in the Here-I-Am mode has deepened. Although in the past I've been delighted when people comment on how young I look, I now tell the "what-will-people-think?" side of myself, "who cares but me how old I look?" And although I'm often aware of the flow of energy that courses through me, I accept that I've only got a limited amount. It will be enough for today's purposes if I measure it well.

Here-I-Am is where I'm at home in myself whether happy or sad, comfortable or sick, upright or slumped, excited or quiet. It's where my truth is.

How'm I doin'? Well, here I am. Come and see.

As James Hollis says in **What Matters Most,** *"We are not here to fit in, be well balanced, or provide exempla for others. We are here to be eccentric, different, perhaps strange, perhaps merely to add our small piece, our little clunky, chunky selves, to the great mosaic of being." What matters most to you?*

Day 1
Your first assignment is to differentiate between the How'm-I-Doin' and the Here-I-Am mode of being during your day. Take notes on how you want others to see you. What do you hope they will think about you? What do you do to help create that impression? What is most important to you in your "presentation?" What aspects of your image of yourself would you like them to see? What do you not want them to know about you?

Day 2
Today make notes on whatever momentarily stops you in your tracks. Whether it's the inexorable hand of fate, as in traffic that delays you on your way to an important appointment, or an unpleasant reaction from your boss, or the unfriendly words of a co-worker — how do you react? Every time you come up against your limitations, you are called back to the present tense as you try to figure out what to do next. Think of such moments as milestones rather than obstacles. Stopping short reminds you of who you are and exactly where you stand.

Day 3
Today, get to know how you present yourself verbally to the world. Imagine there's a little gnome sitting on your shoulder who whispers in your ear every time you say something that's meant to impress people.

Or maybe he giggles with delight every time you put someone "in their place." Let him help you discover which of the comments you make in public are true indications of how you think and feel, which you make in hopes of being overheard and admired, and which are just plain unfriendly. When are you most authentically yourself?

Day 4

Now that you've studied your public and private words, begin to evaluate your actions in the same way. The need to be liked makes us perform in certain ways whenever we feel who we are isn't enough. Your question for today is, what is the motivation for each act you perform as you go through the day? Many of them will be based on necessity, others on duty, still others flow from an open heart. But some will always be geared toward being noticed and admired. Remember that story in the Gospel of Mathew about the man who prayed sanctimoniously in public so all could admire his dedication? Does that ever apply to you?

Day 5

Finally, what is your inner emotional state when you are with other people? How hard do you have to work to be yourself when you are with others? Do you feel exposed? Or delighted to be with company? Do some people make you work harder to be the person you'd like them to think you are? Formulate some aspects of your concern for how others see you and write them down. What could you do or say differently in the name of being more authentic? Where does the inner authority come from that can say "Here I Am?"

Stand Like a Tree

Standing and waiting can be standing fast, getting stuck or holding onto oneself too tightly. But in any case it probably means keeping one's impatience under control. For example, if you're in a line at the bank or waiting for a bus or subway, what to do? There are several possibilities, including impotent fuming and cursing. And one alternative is to look within, to take the time to remember yourself here and now, and hold impatience at bay with a conscious effort to turn your attention elsewhere.

Recently I started practicing "standing like a tree," or Zhan Zhuang, a Qigong exercise I read about in Master Lam Kam Chuen's book, *The Way of Energy*. As Master Lam explains, we are always in motion, our minds endlessly pulled around by stimuli, "a miniature field of the electromagnetic energy of the universe." Standing like a tree works at relaxing both the nervous system and the muscular system in what he terms a "renewed circulation of the original, natural energy in our bodies and minds." And it can be done anywhere, any time you wait around for whatever's next on your list.

Following the author's advice, I stood still five minutes every morning for two weeks, then stepped up to 10 minutes a day. If you're game to try it, stand quietly, feet firmly planted, shoulder width apart. Soften your knees a little and allow the sacrum to drop naturally. As you stand there, tune into what's going on in your body, reminding yourself every so often to let go any holding onto ankles, knees and hips.

Although the exercise may seem passive, as soon as you begin to practice, you will discover how active and demanding it really is. As your whole psycho-physical system lets go into a new balance, you will probably begin to feel some aches, pains and tensions. Welcome them as useful messages, if you can. In fact, they are an important part of the experience, informing you of where you've been tight and which corner of your body is at odds with the whole of yourself.

When I get up in the morning, plans or anxieties about the day may intrude on my ability to attend to the movements of the body and the energy, or *chi*, circulating through it. By standing like a tree, I practice waiting like a seeker, not resolved but questioning, not gripping but exploring. Gradually emotions and physical tensions fade and the mind sharpens, ready to meet the day. I am no longer an unattended vehicle. In the words of Lao Tzu in the *Tao Te Ching*:

> Standing alone and unchanging
> One can observe every mystery
> Present at every moment and ceaselessly continuing —
> This is the gateway to indescribable marvels.

Perhaps the first prerequisite of this quiet work is to accept yourself as you are, so you need to take any weaknesses or injuries into account. When you apply the instructions, let common sense and the wisdom of your body be your guide. While martial art experts practice Zhan Zhuang in order to obtain internal power and dominate their enemies, we ordinary mortals can profit from the physical health and longevity it offers. Many physical imbalances will begin to correct themselves if you practice daily.

Day 1
Stand without moving for three to five minutes at first, feet shoulder width apart, upright but with your knees soft and slightly bent. As you begin, imagine that your feet have roots in the earth, receiving energy from below. Each foot we shove carelessly into our shoes has 26 bones, and together they carry a quarter of all the bones in the body, as well as many of its joints. In spite of this, we are mostly unaware of these two architecturally fascinating structures. As you get to know your feet better, pay special attention to the acupuncture point Kidney One, Yongquan or Bubbling Spring, at the center of the sole of each foot, just behind the arch of frontal bones. Connect with it today. It's your gateway to earth energy.

Day 2

Hopefully you have practiced standing like a tree in the early morning or late in the evening and begin to have a feel for it. Today take the practice into your day. The active inner stillness that you felt as you stood by yourself can be accessed at any time: in meetings, sitting at your desk, waiting for the red light to change, or just waiting around for something to happen. Whenever you stand, sit or walk, try to recall that active yet immobile state, and turn your attention to the impression of energy flowing through your body.

Day 3

The importance of connecting with earth energy may be an unfamiliar idea. We are used to thinking of finer energy coming down from the skies, from Heaven above. But in Tai Chi and Zhan Zhuang the flow of earth energy, as it surges up from below, is just as important. For today, keep the focus of your attention on the sensation of your weight each time you shift from one foot to the other, doing the usual things you do. IF there's a patch of grass nearby, take off your shoes and feel the earth under you in the new/old activity called Earthing. You can even buy an earthing *sheet on the internet and be grounded all night long.*

Day 4

Add a message to your standing practice: think of standing and waiting like a seeker. Ask "How am I?" and "What is my body up to?" every few minutes. That way you gather data for a better understanding of yourself and your vehicle. Why is it so important to do this? Because we forget that although we are standing still, we are always in movement.

You can sense, in a practical way, how everything inside you is also in movement — blood, nerves and muscles. This mini-exercise can leave you feeling quite energized. What's more, perhaps by standing and waiting, an experience of expanding presence within stillness, you may never become impatient again!

Day 5

Taoist concepts are often at odds with our western thinking. For example, in Tai Chi we are taught to retreat in order to advance. How could drawing back instead of insisting on your own way play out in your life today? Taoism also celebrates the power of the yielding to overcome the firm or the liquid to overcome the rigid, just as flowing water gradually wears down a rock or a tsunami destroys everything in its

STAND LIKE A TREE

path. So there's probably more than one way to get what you are determined to have today!

Add a message to your standing practice: think of standing and waiting like a seeker. Ask "How am I?" and "What is my body up to?" every few minutes. That way you gather data for a better understanding of yourself and your vehicle. Why is it so important to do this? Because we forget that although we are standing still, we are always in movement.

You can sense, in a practical way, how everything inside you is also in movement — blood, nerves and muscles. This mini-exercise can leave you feeling quite energized. What's more, perhaps by standing and waiting, an experience of expanding presence within stillness, you may never become impatient again!

Only God Is Perfect

I don't know who said it, but it carries an important message for all of us — about being mortal, being ordinary, being myself. It took me sixty years and the patience of a lot of friends and relatives to absorb this fact into my bones.

From an early age I expected a lot from myself and everybody else. My grade school teachers labeled me "hypercritical" before I knew what the word meant. And from then on, my addiction to perfection just got worse.

Perhaps my children first woke me up to the pretension of my perfectionist demands. In earlier years they attempted to meet some of the impossible standards I had set them and, later, as adults, they watched me stumble and recognize my limitations. Why weren't my high standards good enough? Simply because they were too high. I always thought I knew how high to set the bars, but I myself didn't always make the effort to jump over them.

It took Thomas Merton's measured words to bring in a little light: "It's a very great thing to be little, which is to be myself." Once that message broke through my inner barriers, the evidence began piling up fast and the number of people who became my teachers multiplied. Marion Woodman's *Addiction to Perfection* was the final clincher, informing me that my resolve to seek perfection wasn't a virtue but more like an illness.

I-AM-NOT-PERFECT! I can say it now without guilt or shame. I can even admit to how much time and energy I've wasted trying to build and maintain that perfectionist image. Yet, strangely enough, I sometimes have to remind myself that I'm not a wimp or a numbskull either! That's the shadow of self-accusation that lies hidden in every perfectionist, an inner voice which attacks us for not measuring up.

While it may seem strange that two such opposite attitudes can live side by side in one person, the inner accuser can drive us to the dark side of ourselves, immersing us in self-attack and self-despising. And sometimes the reverse is true: the seemingly humble, helpful, self-abnegating person may well be driven to excessive self-mortification by hidden perfectionist demands. But don't despair. Merton's words can once more draw us out of any confusion: "What am I?" he asks in *No Man Is An Island*, and answers his own question: "I am myself a word spoken by God. Can God speak a word that does not have any meaning?"

Although I used to think of my addiction to perfection as a virtue, Marion Woodman showed me how topsy-turvy was my view. She summed it up elegantly in **The Ravaged Bridegroom:** *"Where perfection is worshipped in consciousness, imperfection is magnetic in the unconscious. Splitting light from dark denies human wholeness." So the choice seems to be either to be perfect or to be whole.*

Day 1
Your first rule as a perfectionist-in-remission is to be careful how and when you set bars for yourself and others. Only set the ones you've already jumped over at least once. And make the jump again each time you suggest that others live by your highest standards or criticize them in your mind. He or she should have done this or that? Do it yourself! And then go to Youtube to listen again to David Roth as he sings, "Don't should on me and I'll not should on you!"

Day 2
Today write in your notebook a description of the event every time you think you are Right, or that someone else is Wrong. Whenever you hear your inner voice criticize someone else, try to return to yourself, to being "just me," or "little ol' me," as I sometimes call myself in an effort to return to reality. It's in your best interest to guard against that image of perfection, because it is tyrannical. It is an enemy of your growth. However, remain alert at those moments when you sincerely give up affirming your Perfectionist side, because self-attack may follow. These are the two poles of the pendulum you swing from. They are not you.

Day 3

Can you find the courage to give up whatever is superfluous in your demands on yourself and others? Try to notice the two extremes of perfectionist and self-attacker, so you can live more often between them, in the pivot point of the pendulum swing. To do this, start by forgiving yourself for not being perfect. Admit to yourself that your dreams exceed your reach and that what you thought was the best path may not be real. Ask yourself, at different moments during the day, "what's really going on under the surface pushme-pullme of my attitude to life?" You may not find an answer, but let the question resound.

Day 4

From pinpricks to major stabs in the heart, forgiveness heals. Detoxify yourself from the Perfectionist tendency today by letting others know you are human. When you say something hurtful, interrupt yourself right away and apologize: "Oops! I didn't mean to say that, and anyway it was mean." Or confess, "For years I've been jealous of your hourglass figure (or your beautiful dresses) because I can't seem to lose weight (or find them)." Or even, "I've always resented the fact that Mother loved you more than the rest of us, but it's not fair to hold you responsible."

Day 5

Acknowledge the Perfectionist in you as a true Terrorist. Name him today. You may never lose him or his partner, the tyrannical inner Persecutor who tells you how worthless you are. But your relationship with them will change as you begin to recognize their activity in you and call them by their real names. It may help you to realize that you are dealing with huge archetypal forces, energies whose power to govern our actions and reactions is greatest when we are blind to them. And although they aren't going to go away, your awareness of their existence will diminish their power over you. It will also change how you respond to life.

Present to My Absence

When I sit down to meditate, I come from a hundred different places in myself and turn for the many thousandth time toward the unknown. What am I doing? Where am I going? Sometimes I think I know. That may mean I'm trying too hard to "get" somewhere I've been before. Maybe I'm reaching for Nirvana, or attempting to repeat yesterday morning's successful connection, or simply wishing to find someplace special in myself where I can feel good. Nothing wrong with feeling good, but trying to get where you are not seldom works. Better to discover where you really are.

It's not easy to give up the longing for a special state. And who doesn't want to soak herself in peace and joy? But by now I've learned that each time I try to meditate I need to go right back to the beginning, back to the recognition that I don't know what to do except let go, and I don't know where to go except where I am. The only certitude is that I've come to the edge of this inner wilderness before.

So here I am — right here, right now — on a fact-finding mission to explore whatever's going on in mind and body. Whatever mood I may be in, my body settles down on the kneeling stool as I begin to sense my mass. Thoughts drag me away, but I call them back and focus on my legs, my belly, my back, the sense of weight, the nooks and crannies of me that are in different states of tension or relaxation.

Whenever I discover I was dozing, or that my thoughts carried me far away, I return again to the assignment — to being here-and-now in this vehicle that I also am. At last the strident needs or plans that were gripping me begin to release their hold. Any exercises or efforts I may have engaged in as I tried to center myself can fall away as the ego gives up its clutch.

A new level of difficulty begins. As I enter into a state of gradually deepening quiet, how not to interfere? My little comments and secret judgments on how well this meditation is going still hover on the sidelines, attempting to capture my attention in a tug of war with a gathering sense of presence. Gradually I become aware of a greater unknown in my present inner reality. Who am I? That or this? How to be truly available to my Self?

If sitting meditation is new to you, experiment with any of the suggestions available in books or on the web, because exploration is the only way you'll find what works best for you. Books and spiritual advisors may suggest you count breaths, chant, visualize, or use other means, but no magic will get you where you want to go. Rather, think of a meditation as a mystery you seek to penetrate by giving up everything that stands in the way. Above all, the ego must yield its sway, and it's not very enthusiastic about doing that!

Day 1
As a first step, when you sit down, begin to question yourself as to what in heaven's name you came here to do. Seek to contact again the need for quiet that brought you to your knees, so to speak. Perhaps you were clear last night about why you wanted to meditate but this morning your intention is weak. Not to worry. Just accept the lack of clarity, and be present to what you feel right now. Your wish is still there somewhere or you'd just get up and go!

Day 2
Your body is your friend, perhaps your best friend. And this is especially true in efforts at meditation. Finding a connection with it is the next step, because your mind and emotions have a life of their own. Your thoughts can roam from here to China and back. Your emotions can blow hot and cold and everything in between. But your body is here in real time. Begin to explore the sensation of your weight on the floor or chair. How much do you weigh? Can you sense that on the ground? Remind yourself that you don't have to hold onto yourself because the earth comes up under you to support you.

Day 3
Mind and breath are keys to the next level. Focus your thoughts step by

step on the different parts of your body. Slowly investigate the state of tension in every inch of you as you scan yourself from feet to head, beginning with how your weight sinks into the floor. Notice what parts of you are touching it. Everything you touch touches you back, just as everything you push, pushes back. (This is true on every level from the material to the psychological to the spiritual.) Then scan your lower and upper legs, moving slowly up your body to include the belly, chest and back, your arms and finally your head.

Day 4

Another day start from the top. Imagine the warmth of the sun beaming down on your head, gradually melting the numbness in your brain and forehead. (By numbness I mean a lack of awareness as well as of sensation, because although we are always caught up in our thoughts, we seldom have a physical sense of the place from which they arise.) Next, see if you can release any tension in the eyes — the juicy organs that run through to the back of your head, where the visual cortex occupies about a third of your cerebral cortex. Then slowly explore the sensation of your cheeks, nose, mouth, and ears. Let your tongue relax as you release the jaw or become aware of how tight it is. Remind yourself that you are not your face — it sits in front of you. Then continue downward to scan your chest, arms, back, belly and legs.

Day 5

Once you are connected with your living body, a sense of your own presence will deepen — you, here and now. As it spreads through you, you can begin to turn your attention to the larger inner landscape in which soul and spirit live. This is the stage of meeting the Other and accepting the unknown. Now your plans, anxieties, inner exercises, and even your ideals can dissolve into the quiet of being your Self.

Loving the Child Within

I was in my fifties when I woke up to the existence of an inner child. Before that, I met any manifestation of innocence, vulnerability or sense of inadequacy in myself with scorn. Any show of weakness threatened to damage the walls of the fortress I'd constructed long ago to protect myself from the blows of life. Nevertheless, once I was able to accept that there was indeed a child essence within me, I realized that while those walls kept others out, they also hemmed me in.

My Superwoman persona had marginalized this tender growing shoot of my essential Self, which it judged as naïve, slow, and inadequate to the task. As I grew up, Superwoman protected me from a war-torn world I found hard to understand, and later helped me provide for myself and three children as a single mother. But when my life began to generate more pressure than I could bear, complaining messages from within assailed me. That was when I began to dialogue with my inner personas. (For more on this, see my book, *Taming Your Inner Tyrant*.)

Why had any manifestation of uncertainty annoyed me so? Why did I call it weakness, and hate so much to make mistakes, needing to prove myself again and again? Why were those precious vestiges of childhood — innocence and openness — so threatening? Most of all, why did I shout at that sensitive side of myself and criticize her when, in fact, she was trying to do her best?

Perhaps you too carry a stern inner judge who considers any frightened or playful part of you childish and unacceptable, meeting it with annoyance or disdain. Life experience may have created a widening gap between this child essence and that Implacable Judge, sometimes referred to as the Superego. What's important is not to allow his sneers to turn you away from the delicate attempt to connect with parts of yourself he refuses to

144

believe in. Pay no attention to his catcalls. Remember, he's just another personality fragment, even though he always thinks he's in charge!

You might suppose, as I did at first, that this delicate soul-part of our essential nature is simply one more fragment, but in *The Archetypes and the Collective Unconscious,* Jung tells us otherwise: "It is a striking paradox in all child myths that the 'child' is on the one hand delivered helpless into the power of terrible enemies and in continual danger of extinction, while on the other he possesses powers far exceeding those of ordinary humanity. This is closely related to the fact that though the child may be 'insignificant,' unknown, 'a mere child,' he is also divine."

That divine child is still alive in us. Learn to care for it.

Christ invites us to "become as a little child." The Taoists suggest we cultivate such an attitude all through our lives. But in spite of the fact that we tend to smile fondly whenever we see a child at work or play, there often isn't much room in our busy world for innocence or an open mind.

Day 1
To discover your own inner child, start by exploring how she expresses herself in you. A child has many moods, a lot of fear, and a sense of adventure. On the one hand, she finds the world new and exciting but, on the other, she is easily overwhelmed. When are you overwhelmed? Call up some memories of your childhood, the happy ones, the sad ones, the angry ones. Which scenes immediately come to mind? What images from the past still have the power to make you angry? Or sad? Or happy? Write them down.

Day 2
Begin to listen to any comments you make secretly to yourself, no matter if they are judgmental, gleeful, snide, relieved, or repressive. Don't criticize them; just write down what you heard. After a while you might even try to answer back. Maybe you'll hear a reply as I did. Little by little (or all of a sudden), a dialogue could begin with a marginalized part of yourself. Don't dwell on it. Don't force it. Our personas don't respond to the demandingness of the ego, and a deeply hurt child must

be treated gently. Listen to his or her complaints. Try to elicit a further response.

Day 3

This attempt to dialogue with an inner persona is a Jungian exercise called Active Imagination. You can try it, as I did, by asking questions and writing down the answers. However, many people find it easier to tune into this mysterious inner world through painting, sculpture, music, or dance. Whatever medium feels right to you, you'll probably discover that the challenge is always the same: your conscious mind will try to dominate, correct or deny any manifestations that appear. But you need to focus more on whatever's flowing from an unknown source, so that an unfamiliar part of yourself can manifest while you watch.

Day 4

That Implacable Judge, who thinks he's the voice of your conscience, is your number one enemy in this endeavor. If you sometimes judge yourself inadequate to the task you are trying to fulfill, pull back from scolding yourself. Ask yourself "who is the judge, and whom am I judging?" When your inner critic attacks the child-self, beware. You don't want to foster a negative relationship — you annoyed and the child-self fearful and confused. She doesn't need an angry critic. She needs you to care about her, but also remind her from time to time of what you consider important. Ask yourself each time you attack yourself for forgetting something, "Who would treat a living child in the accusing way I sometimes treat myself?"

Day 5

Another approach to understanding the child-self is to become more aware of your body language. Body and child are closely related, so how the body reacts to whatever's going on offers clues to the child's point of view. For example, at any moment when you feel good or bad today, ask yourself why. And who in you feels good? Who wants to cry? Why did you suddenly smile just now? Or frown? Notice the moments that make you want to dance. Or sing.

Getting It All Together

Without a cordial relation between the mind and the body, either mental confusion or an aching body may be in store. As the ancient Taoist Song of the Thirteen Positions says, "The mind and Chi direct, and the flesh and bones follow." The bones are there to maintain our structure and carry our weight. The muscles are there to help us move around and do stuff. And the nervous system offers a never-ending dialogue between the body and the brain.

They say the Chi, our life energy, lives in the blood. Somewhat disorganized, it needs to be directed by our thought. In fact, since energy follows thought, it will flow wherever our thoughts go. As Deepak Chopra explains it, "The blood is not a chemical soup; it is a multi-lane freeway in which thousands of messages, conveyed by hormones, neuropeptides, immune cells and enzymes, are forever traveling, each intent on a mission, each capable of maintaining its own integrity as an impulse of intelligence."

However, a thousand thoughts invade my inner space every minute — things I should do, want to do, problems and solutions, dreams of glory. And there's only one body here, in real time, doing its best in spite of all the burdens with which I weigh it down. It cannot possibly meet this multiplicity of demands. Why? Because it can only do one thing at a time.

The body lives in the present tense. And what could be better if I wish to be present? But instead of relating to it, I hurry, push, and propel it forward, pressuring it to accomplish as much as possible as fast as it possibly can. Inevitably it will become exhausted and even angry. And sooner or later it will break down.

Maybe you think I exaggerate the importance of an equal partnership. Perhaps you haven't noticed that your body feels relief when it's treated with respect. Let me share today's discovery: After a busy morning at the computer, I headed out for a quick walk in the Park, still grappling with unsolved issues. As I approached the trees, my body relaxed and expanded so quickly that the letting go was a shock. What's more, I realized I was smiling. Go figure!

Another example: I recently sang Mozart's Coronation Mass with a chorus 120 voices strong. The next day my whole body vibrated with energy, my movements were free and flowing, and my automatic-thought machinery, which usually mutters reminders from my To-Do list, kept on repeating: "Glorificamos Te!"

How to make a new relationship with your vehicle under difficult circumstances or when you are stressed out? For example, let's say you sit at home or in your office chair, in front of a computer, or at a meeting, a concert, a school performance by one of your kids, or even in church. Perhaps you're bored or just too tired. How to crank up your attention enough to get the job done, listen intelligently to your companions or avoid embarrassing your family by snoring at the show?

Step 1

Here's what you could try: Sit up straight on the edge of your chair for a moment. Notice how your weight rests on your sit-bones at the base of the torso (sit on your hands for a moment to find these two bony protuberances). Then follow the spine as it rises up from them, visualizing it like a ladder you could clamber up on tiny imaginary feet, vertebra by vertebra (24 of them), to the top.

Step 2

There you are, focused on the top vertebra, the Atlas, which is higher than you might think, behind your eyes and between your ears. Your head is lightly balanced on it. Once you're up there, think intentionally about the opposite direction, all the way back down again to the sit-bones. In fact, it's often useful to think in two directions at once — in this case, of your head floating up off your spine as your sit-bones sink deep into the chair. The spine will lengthen with this thought and you may begin to relax and feel energized as well.

Step 3

Close your eyes and ask yourself a series of questions. First, "What's under my chair?" Try to see it in your mind's eye, without actually bending over and looking. Maybe there's a candy wrapper, maybe your briefcase, umbrella, or the bag of stuff you bought on the way there. Or maybe you have no idea!

Step 4

Then bring your mind's eye out from under the seat as you open your awareness to whatever's on your left, without turning to look. Maybe it's another chair where a person you like, or don't like, or don't know, is sitting. What's she wearing? Then, after a minute or two, shift the focus of your attention to the space on your right. Let that impression come into your consciousness, remembering what you saw there as best you can. Next, focus on what's above you. Maybe there's a balcony up there under high ceilings and lights, or a low ceiling — what color is it?

Step 5

Finally, bring to mind as clear an image as possible of what you think is behind you. You don't actually turn your head to see, because you're trying to remember what you saw earlier. "Hmm. Was I paying attention?" And at the very end, recall what was in front of you. That's where we live most of the time. It usually eats up all our attention. Open your eyes and check out all these directions to see how much you remembered. Then ask yourself, "Am I still stressed, sleepy, bored, uncomfortable?" and silently try to describe how you feel right now.

The Wages of Fear

President Franklin D. Roosevelt is widely quoted as saying, in the depths of the Depression, "The only thing we have to fear is fear itself." It has become a truism, but is it really true? Or is fear built into the foundation and even the bony structure of our lives.

In early childhood we learn to fear the unknown and the unexpected: the noise we don't recognize, the slap we didn't know we "deserved," the danger we hadn't enough experience to be wary of, the pain that makes no sense. Thus from our early years, surprise breeds fear in us. No wonder the child often grows into a cautious, suspicious adult, resistant to change! And our fear is kept alive by further unanticipated suffering as we grow older. Threats and new shocks prove to us again and again that what's unknown can be painful and dangerous.

"Fine," you might ask, "but how about explorers and daredevils?" They do seem to be on another track, but maybe they are simply at the other end of the same stick — their courage fueled by an inner compulsion to press against the boundaries of fear, to test themselves against extreme danger. Or, on the other hand, perhaps they feel safer than we do, protected by a greater presence than their own.

In any case, let's agree that something resists change and opposes risk in most of us. The question is, how to live so that this habitual tendency, developed for whatever reason into a dominant unconscious attitude, doesn't block out the nourishment we want and need from life. Am I afraid to start again, marry again, take a new job in a new field, play a new game? Am I holding myself back — not allowing a full expression of myself, nor taking advantage of all the joys and discoveries life can offer?

If my deepest wish is to affirm my development into the person I was meant to be, I need to let go into life in spite of my instinctive fear of the unknown. So maybe you'll join me in listening one more time to the theme song from the movie Working Girl: "Let the river run!"

Do you wonder where your energy has gone when you are afraid? We need energy to meet the demands of life, but that same energy seems to disappear when we're frightened. Nevertheless, it's still there, hidden away in the reaction itself. And, in my experience, it can only be summoned back when you admit to being afraid.

Day 1
Although we desperately want to live in a state of certainty, we seldom know what the result of our actions will be, or even what's going to happen next. This produces an unconscious anxiety that can develop into a general attitude to life. If real fear fills you when you are confronted by a thug on a dark street, anxiety is dread of future threats, such as when you hear footsteps behind you and don't know whose they are. So, today, at any moment you feel nervous, try to figure out which it is, fear or anxiety.

Day 2
Today turn the searchlight of your mind's attention fully on whatever anxious or scary situation you may find yourself in. Your attention is powerful. It can help you face the devil himself. Let your mind clarify the threat itself as well as the bodily sensations that have appeared along with it. Name the threat out loud, as in "I thought my boss was going to come down on me but all he wanted was some envelopes." Then get up and stretch your arms overhead, connecting your fingertips to the bottom of your feet in your mind.

Day 3
You've probably already noticed that, as with all emotions, fear and anxiety express themselves in the body. You know you are afraid because of your pounding heart, gooseflesh, churning stomach, sweaty armpits, and perhaps a sense of weakness and inability to cope. One way to move out of the overwhelmment of that state is to shift your attention away from the emotional reaction and become the witness of your physical sensations. As you name each sensation gathered around the reaction of fear, you move away from the feeling of helplessness and toward taking

the necessary action. It also invites you to focus on where the suffering is actually taking place.

Day 4
In situations of fear or helplessness, begin to differentiate between internal and external fears. Are you afraid for your life or is your self-image threatened? The ego doesn't like to be pushed into a corner, made to feel small, but sometimes we are suffused with self-doubt and power-lessness, even shame. Situations I can't control, or in which I feel powerless, inevitably induce fear, but there's a big difference between that thug in the street and the boss I'm sure is about to fire me. Both signify a situation I can't control, but while one threatens my very existence, the other only threatens my life-as-it-is.

Day 5
Those of us who believe in a higher power or an intelligent universe have a further source to call on for help. You may be like me — always want to go it alone, solve your own problems, face your fears and anxieties and hold fast. But when I'm really up against it, like the moment I was halfway up the almost vertical wall of a cliff and the shale began to crumble under my feet, or when I have such a sense of desolation and loss that I can barely go on, I turn for help. And there is always help when we're at the end of our tether. Why not turn more often to your deeper Self? Turn today.

The Enemy Within

In the study of Tai Chi as in life, an inner enemy is always present. You can call it the devil, or our lesser self, or whatever you want, but something opposes our efforts and intentions, skewing us away from what we are determined to accomplish. When Master T. T. Liang told me about the enemy who appears each time I practice the Tai Chi Solo Exercise, he said it was up to me to discover it for myself.

Because Tai Chi is a martial art, I expected to practice sometimes in a twosome. But the suggestion that I must do battle alone with an inner opponent came as a surprise. So I began to pay attention as I went through the forms. First I noticed how, as I struggled to focus on the accuracy of the positions and the flow of energy, my thoughts continually wandered away. Then I saw how, when Master Liang was there, or people watched me in the park, I focused carefully on what I was doing. But when no one was around to observe my effort or my accuracy, I took it easy.

Years later I discovered yet another adversary — that demanding Perfectionist I've written about in Only God is Perfect, who calls me names any time I don't correspond to his rules. He may shout "Stupid!" if I drop something or "There you go again!" when I forget something I meant to take with me. Whatever his message, he's always alert to point out that I'm too slow, too confused, too forgetful, too tired, too old.

What I lose, what we all lose, each time we accept the opinion of this persecutor in the psyche, is a sense of who we are. Each of us has a rhythm that's our own, and when connected to it, we are centered in ourselves. Practicing Tai Chi helps us to find that rhythm. But the knife-sharp stabs of the accuser throw us off our balance and into self-doubt.

People often talk about their rights, even become indignant when those rights are threatened. Then why is it so hard to remember that I have the right to be me and you have the right to be you? Why do we cling to this impossible image of perfect me or perfect you or listen to this inner tyrant who wants to make us over into someone else? Surely oughts and shoulds are words the enemy uses to confuse us and throw us off balance. They have nothing to do with the continuing movement of life in which we attempt to find our own unique rhythm. My job isn't to practice perfection, but to learn how to be me — just as you might learn how to be you.

In this attempt to meet the enemy within, your best friend is your body. I tried just now, as my turning thoughts took me away from what I was doing, to focus on my weight on the ground. Then I sensed the Ocean of Chi in my belly and visualized a column of golden light pulsing up my spine. Suddenly I was all there, engaged in getting the job done. Try it for yourself.

Day 1
Decide how you want to dedicate your time today. Clarify your aim, whatever it may be, by saying it out loud several times, and make an effort to honor your decision. Then notice whatever opposes your attending to it. What pulls you away or gets in the way? At the end of the day, write down both your original aim and whatever came along to oppose it, as well as what finally happened.

Day 2
Clear thinking is essential to help you carry out your aims. But thoughts can also serve as impediments. They may intrude on your intention, pulling you away to some future plan, a past incident, or even what's for dinner. You can't stop your thoughts, but you can learn to let them pass through you like clouds moving across the sky. Each time irrelevant thoughts interrupt your aims today, say out loud, "I am not my thoughts," and return to your effort.

Day 3
Another approach when turning thoughts or insistent inner arguments interfere with what you have in hand, is to access your feet. The vibrant flesh, warm blood and 26 bones in each foot carry you around wherever you want to go. Visit them today for a moment before you begin the task

you set out for yourself, then spend your time connected to them as they move you around. At the end of the day, thank them for their hard work these many years by massaging them gently with a sweet-smelling oil.

Day 4
Another pervasive enemy of your concentration comes from your emotional nature. When anxiety interferes with your effort, remind yourself that it is never about present reality. It's always about past happenings or fears of what could happen in the future. Tell yourself often, out loud, "I wish to be here, right now, right where I am," and listen closely to the vibration of your voice as you say it. Speaking your aim out loud can be a powerful affirmation.

Day 5
Perhaps, in the middle of what you are doing, a part of you may act out like a sullen teenager who says whiningly, "But I don't feeel like it!" That's ok. Maybe you are sick, tired, or forcing something on yourself. If so, make an intentional appointment with yourself to continue your task in the near future. But if you need to finish the job right away, how to deal with that unruly rebel inside? Begin a dialogue. Give him (or her) room to express himself. Ask him what he wants to do instead, then decide if that's what you would like to do as well. Otherwise ask him to wait till later, promising him an opportunity at another time.

There is no Wealth but Life

Are you muttering a sarcastic comment as you read this quote from 19th century art critic John Ruskin? It's undoubtedly true that life could be a lot pleasanter with wealth than without it. Money can buy comfort in a thousand forms, and fun in a million ways. It can even buy happiness sometimes, although that depends on what makes you happy and for how long it keeps you satisfied. But buy life? That's quite another story.

Where does life come from and where does it go when it disappears? Not only the physical life of birth and death, but the life energy that pulsates in us, resounds through us, and out of which we say "I feel good." Or that eludes us when we complain "I feel sooooo tired!" Energy fires me up every morning, to a greater or lesser degree, no matter how tired I was the night before. It allows me to sympathize, love or get annoyed at you with all my juices. It also permits me to write a book, go running, build a bridge or study neuroscience.

Nobody really seems to know what energy actually is, although there are a lot of words to explain it. We do know through experience that we wake up every morning sometimes almost boundlessly energized, sometimes lost in the aftertaste of an unpleasant dream or tied up in anxiety about a problem that must be solved. And all through the day we experience ourselves either as able to meet whatever's going on, or too tired to follow through, or too angry or discouraged to concentrate.

Somewhere in all this is a key to what really makes us tick. For whether I'm aware of it or not, the state of my energy — the quality of my secret inner love affair with each moment as I live it — determines how I feel. As energy plays through the world of my body, mind and feelings, I am offered the richness of my days and hours, the nourishment to feel good about myself, to decide, accept, and refuse. Or, on the contrary, my energy can vanish, leaving me impoverished, drained, unable to cope.

My state of energy also governs my decisions. At any given moment I must decide what I want and what I'm prepared to pay for it — a cup of coffee, a nap, a purchase on the stock market, or a game with a grandchild. Or it may insist that I give up all that and pay attention to the need for rest.

Our thoughts and imagination seem to run on forever, powered by an unknown jet fuel. They never seem to stop. But we can experience quite clearly how our physical energy peters out when we are unable to get through our tasks. In such moments, how we long for a new access of energy, a sense of ease and the ability to finish whatever we're engaged in.

Day 1
Begin to pay more attention to your state of energy at any given moment. How energized did you feel when you got up this morning, for example? And how was your energy level after a shower or a cup of coffee? Start to track the subtle and not-so-subtle changes today. Write them down. Imagine that you are checking the temperature on a thermometer to see what the weather's like outside. What's your own inner weather right now? Let's call it your Energy Thermometer or ET. Investigate it at various moments in the day.

Day 2
Now that you've practiced noticing changes with your inner thermometer for a day, let's change the game. This time, check your ET at specific times, like every two hours, or any time you go in and out of a particular room. Discover how often a shift takes place, sometimes major, sometimes minor.

Day 3
Today let's add a new thermometer that registers how you feel. We'll call it the EMT as in Emotional Mood Thermometer. Notice whenever your mood shifts. When do you feel sad, happy, bored, or excited? Follow both your ET and EMT throughout the day, as many times as you remember, noting down the time of day and a brief description of what's going on.

Day 4

Now let's put the two thermometers together. What relationship, if any, does your ET have with your EMT at different times and in different activities? How does either of them change after you get up off your chair and begin to move around, or when you have something to eat, or meet a friend? Find out which activities simultaneously engage mind and body and make notes on how their convergence influences both your energy level and your emotional mood.

Day 5

Finally, ask yourself often during the day what ET or EMT you would prefer to spend the time of your life in. Once you've clarified that, explore how much you are prepared to pay each time for the privilege. The answer could change your life.

Ego and Ocean

What a delight to walk on the beach or gaze out of this picture window at the movement of the water! Every January I get to spend Two Wonderful Weeks at the Manasota Beach Club in Florida. I occupy a gorgeous suite overlooking the Gulf while I de-stress from New York life as I eat gourmet food, and teach Tai Chi and the Alexander Technique.

It's a joy to be so close to the sea. Poets love to write about it, while we ordinary mortals simply lie on the beach and watch the waves roll in. I can stay there for hours, mesmerized by their movement as they roll up on the sand, then get sucked back into the heart of ocean, only to flow back toward me a moment later. Like the water that is creeping toward my feet right now, those waves are always new.

Last night I watched the ocean glisten under a full moon, and thought about that endless repetition, which is at the same time always new. The waves are like the Ego, foaming, spraying, continually calling attention to themselves: "Yaayy!" they say. And "Look at me, way up here!" Then they fall back into the ocean and disappear.

But the ocean itself isn't like that at all. It has a powerful "I AM," which it affirms without effort. No need to call attention to itself. The waves are only the surface life of something much deeper and greater. That realization calls me back to myself as I ask, "Am I so caught up in the momentary movements of my life, its wants and lacks, that I forget the larger whole I'm part of, the Self in me?"

Like waves and ocean, Ego and Self are always in movement, in my thoughts, my emotional reactions, and my life of accomplishments. But mind, body and being sometimes need to let go of movement and busyness in order to refresh themselves. They need to connect with a deeper resonance that's always there, waiting to be heard. Just as waves fold themselves back into the source of their energy, the ocean, I too can return to the endlessly elusive present moment in which I AM – HERE – NOW. And just as waves are servant to ocean, I am here to serve the Self in me.

The path to freedom from the incessant demands of the ego is through recognition of another life in me, beyond my comprehension. Not that a strong ego isn't important to serve the needs of the world and your own, but that it must take its place within a larger context. It is here to serve Great Nature, and your true Self. In an ancient Zuni ritual, an egoistic craving or self-affirmation is pulled away from that central place where, at any given moment, it tries to dominate the whole of ourselves, and hooked onto our backside, where perhaps once we had a tail. Whenever it is needed again to represent us, we can unhook it and bring it back into action.

Day 1
What is it about you that you think communicates to the world who you are — the logo on your shirt, the smile on your face, the strictness of your self discipline, or the openness of your heart? Notice today, any time your path crosses that of another person, what part of you comes into play — the pleaser, the critic, the know-it-all, or the interested human being.

Day 2
Great Nature and our own nature are telling us who we are 24 hours a day. Tune into any form of outer nature you meet, from tree or flower to an insect crawling across your kitchen floor. If nothing comes across your path, buy a plant. As you water it, listen to it as if you could almost hear what it's saying. You might even discover you have something to say in reply.

Day 3
One way to return to your Self, to the ground of your Being, is through stillness — sitting in meditation and listening to your inner life. But because energy is always in movement, you can also find your way to it through movement. A runner's high or an athlete's zone is devoid of ego while they are in action. No time for it. Experiment with how to find

*freedom from the ego's drive today as you concentrate on your move-
ments in a dedicated manner.*

Day 4
*There's nothing wrong with a strong ego — it helps you carry your
intention through to the end. It allows you to interact with the world.
But today, when you are with other people, look inside to see if you can
differentiate between an ego impulse such as "Hey, guys, look at me!"
and a sense of communion, as in "I so enjoy being here together with
you." And why not bring joy with a small gift to a friend or neighbor.
The act of giving lights another part of us, the part that knows it is here
to serve. What does the ego serve, and whom do you serve?*

Day 5
*In order to find your way to that powerful I AM, you need to move
beyond personal ego affirmation for a little while and join the larger
ocean of Being. Its current flows through you all the time but you are
seldom aware of it. Sitting quietly, listening to the world and yourself,
you may find your way there. On a mountaintop or at the edge of the
sea, or face to face with a great tree, it may come by itself. It is also
expressed in the generosity of real human love. Try to connect with that
great current today, any way you can. As the Upanishads say, "This
Self is the honey of all beings, and all beings are the honey of this Self."
As this year of our working together comes to a close, I hope you have
found much in these reflections and exercises to deepen your connection
to that Self.*

Bibliography

Dear reader: The books on this list have been integral to my own search for understanding. Some of them are mentioned in the text. All of them have guided me in one way or another and will perhaps be useful to you. The slim volumes marked with a single asterisk might inspire you at the breakfast table. I always read a few pages along with my morning tea, because wise and provocative ideas help me enter the coming day in a more whole way. Those with two asterisks can be fine breakfast reading as well and, depending on where your interests lie, are useful study guides for practical exploration.

Alexander, F. Matthias, *The Use of the Self*, Orion Publishing Group, UK, 2002.

Benoit, Hubert, *Let Go! Theory and Practice of Detachment According to Zen*, translated by Albert Low, Allen & Unwin, London, 1962.**

The Bhagavad-Gita: The Song of God, translated and with commentaries by Swami Prabhavananda and Christopher Isherwood, Signet Classics, New York, 2002.*

Blake, William, *Songs of Innocence and Experience*, Abrams, New York, 2007.

Borysenko, Joan, *Minding the Body, Mending the Mind*, Bantam Books, New York, 1993.**

———. *Inner Peace for Busy People: 52 Simple Strategies for Transforming Your Life*, Hay House, Carlesbad CA, 2001.*

Brillat-Savarin, Jean Anthelme, *Physiology of Taste, or Meditations on Transcendental Gastronomy*, translated by M. F. K. Fisher, The Heritage Press, New York, 1949

Brother Lawrence, *The Practice of the Presence of God*, Hendrickson Publications, Peabody MA, 2004.*

Buber, Martin, *I and Thou*, translated by Ronald Gregor Smith, Continuum International Publishing Group, London, 1984.**

———. *The Way of Man: According to the Teaching of Hasidism*, Citadel Press, New York, 1996.*

Cameron, Julia, *The Artist's Way: A Spiritual Path to Higher Creativity*, Jeremy P. Tarcher, New York, 2002.**

Campbell, Joseph, *The Hero With a Thousand Faces*, Princeton University Press, NJ, 1990.

Chopra, Deepak, *Quantum Healing: Exploring the Frontiers of Mind/Body Medicine*, Bantam Books, New York, 1990.

———. *Ageless Body, Timeless Mind: The Quantum Alternative to Growing Old*, Harmony Books, New York, 1993.**

The Cloud of Unknowing: The Classic of Medieval Mysticism (Foreword by Evelyn Underhill), Kessinger Publishing, Whitefish MT, 1998.*

Cohen, Gene D., *The Creative Age: Awakening Human Potential in the Second Half of Life*, HarperCollins, New York, 2000.**

Coomeraswamy, Ananda, *The Dance of Shiva: On Indian Art and Culture*, Noonday Press/Farrar, Straus and Giroux, New York, 1974.**

Corbin, Henry, *Alone with the Alone: Creative Imagination in the Sufism of Ibn 'Arabi*, translated by R. Manheim, Princeton University Press, NJ, 1998.

———. *Avicenna and the Visionary Recital*, translated by Willard R. Trask, Bollingen Series Pantheon Books, New York, 1960.

Daumal, René, *Mount Analogue: A Novel of Symbolically Authentic Non-Euclidean Adventures in Mountain Climbing*, translated by Roger Shattuck, City Lights Books, San Francisco,1968.*

De Chardin, Teilhard, *The Human Phenomenon*, translated by Sarah Appleton-Weber, Sussex Academic Press, Brighton UK, 2003.

De Llosa, Patty, *The Practice of Presence: Five Paths for Daily Life*, Morning Light Press, Sandpoint ID, 2006

———. *Taming Your Inner Tyrant: A Path to Healing Through Dialogues with Oneself*, A Spiritual Evolution Press, Holmdel NJ, 2011.

De Salzmann, Jeanne, *The Reality of Being: The Fourth Way of Gurdjieff*, Shambhala Boston, 2010.

De Salzmann, Michel, *Man's Ever New and Eternal Challenge*, article in *On the Way to Self Knowledge*. New York: Alfred A. Knopf, 1976, pp. 54-83.

Dhammapada: The Sayings of the Buddha, translated by Thomas Byrom, Harmony/Bell Tower, New York, 2001.*

Doidge, Norman, *The Brain that Changes Itself: Stories of Personal Triumph from the Frontiers of Brain Science*, Penguin Books, New York, 2007.**

Edinger, Edward, *Ego and Archetype: Individuation and the Religious Function of the Psyche*, Shambhala, Boston, 1992.**

———. *The Creation of Consciousness: Jung's Myth for Modern Man*, Inner City Books, l984.*

Eliot, T. S., *The Complete Poems and Plays 1909–1950*, Harcourt Brace, New York, 1952.

Epstein, Mark, *Thoughts without a Thinker: Psychotherapy from a Buddhist Perspective*, Basic Books, New York, l995.**

Farid ud-Din Attar, *The Conference of the Birds*, translated by Garcin de Tassy into French and by C.S. Nott into English, Lowe and Brydone, London, 1954.*

Feldenkrais, Moishe, *The Potent Self: A Guide to Spontaneity*, Harper & Row, New York, 1985.**

Gibran, Khalil, *The Prophet*, Random House, New York, 1997.

The Gospel of Mary Magdalene: Jesus and the First Woman Apostle, translated into French with commentary by Jean-Ives Leloup (translated from French to English by Joseph Rowe), Inner Traditions International, Rochester VT, 2002.*

The Gospel of Thomas: The Hidden Sayings of Jesus, translated by Marvin W. Meyer with commentary by Harold Bloom, Harper San Francisco, 1993.*

Greenspan, Miriam, *Healing through the Dark Emotions: The Wisdom of Grief, Fear, and Despair*, Shambhala, Boston, 2003.**

Guggenbuhl-Craig, Adolf, *Power in the Helping Professions*, Spring Publications, New York, 1998

Gurdjieff, G. I., *Beelzebub's Tales to His Grandson*, Viking Arkana, New York, 1992. Audiotape available in MP3 format from Traditional Studies Press, Toronto, Canada at www.TraditionalStudiesPress.com.

———. *Meetings with Remarkable Men*, E.P. Dutton, New York, 1974.**

———. *Life is Real Only Then When "I Am,"* E.P. Dutton, New York, 1982.

———. *Views from the Real World: Early Talks of Gurdjieff*, Viking Press, New York, 1991.**

Gurdjieff: Essays and Reflections on the Man and His Teaching, Jacob Needleman and George Baker (editors), Continuum Press, New York, 1996.**

The Hermetica: The Lost Wisdom of the Pharaohs, translated by Timothy Freke and Peter Gandy, Jeremy P. Tarcher/Putnam, New York, 1999.*

Herrigel, Eugene, *Zen in the Art of Archery*, Vintage Books, New York, 1999.*

Hesse, Herman, *Siddhartha*, New Directions, New York, 1951.*

Hillman, James, *The Soul's Code: In Search of Character and Calling*, Warner Books, New York, 1997.**

———. *The Thought of the Heart and the Soul of the World*, Spring Publications, Woodstock CT, 1997.*

Hollis, James, *What Matters Most: Living a More Considered Life*, Gotham, New York, 2009.**

———. *Why Good People do Bad Things: Understanding Our Darker Selves*, Gotham, New York, 2007.**

———. *Swamplands of the Soul: New Life in Dismal Places*, Inner City Books, Toronto, 1996.**

Hopkins, Gerard Manley, *Poems*, Humphrey Milford, London, 1918

The I Ching: or Book of Changes, translated into German by Richard Wilhelm, and into English by Cary F. Baynes, Princeton University Press, NJ, 1970.**

Iyengar, B. K. S., *Light on the Yoga Sutras of Patanjali*, Thorsons Publishers, New York, 2003.**

Johnson, Robert, *Inner Work: Using Dreams and Creative Imagination for Personal Growth and Integration*, HarperCollins, New York, 1986.**

———. *Inner Gold: Understanding Psychological Projection*, Koa Books, Kihei Hawaii, 2008.*

Johnson, Robert, with Jerry Ruhl, *Living Your Unlived Life: Coping with Unrealized Dreams and Fulfilling Your Purpose in the Second Half of Life*, Tarcher, New York, 2007.*

Jung, C. G., *The Collected Works of C.G. Jung*, edited by H. Read, M. Fordham, G. Adler, and W. McGuire, 20 Volumes. Bollingen Series XX, Princeton University Press, NJ, 1992.

———. *Memories, Dreams, Reflections*, Vintage Books, New York, 1989.**

———. *Modern Man in Search of a Soul*, Harcourt Trade Publications, New York, 1995.**

Jung on Active Imagination, Edited and with an introduction by Joan Chodorow, Princeton University Press, NJ, 1997.**

Kabat-Zinn, Jon, *Wherever You Go, There You Are: Mindfulness Meditation in Everyday Life*, Hyperion, New York, 1994.*

Kalsched, Donald, *Trauma and the Soul: A Psycho-spiritual Approach to Human Development and its Interruption*, Routledge, New York, 2013.**

Kam-Chuen, Lam, *The Way of Energy: Mastering the Chinese Art of Internal Strength with Chi Kung Exercise*, Gaia Books, New York, 1991.**

Keating, Thomas, *Open Mind, Open Heart: The Contemplative Dimension of the Gospel*, Continuum Press, New York, 2004.**

Kierkegaard, Soren, *Purity of Heart is to Will One Thing*, Harper & Row, New York, 1956.

Klein, Jean, *The Ease of Being*, Acorn Press, Durham, NC, 1986.*

Krishnamurti, *The Flame of Attention*, Harper & Row, New York, 1984.*

——. *Beyond Violence*, Gollancz, London, 1973.**

Lannes, Henriette, *This Fundamental Quest: The Journey of a Pupil of G. I. Gurdjieff*, Far West Institute, San Francisco, 2006.**

Lao Tsu, *The Tao Te Ching*, translation by Gia Fu Feng and Jane English, Vintage Books, New York, 1997.*

Lehrhaupt, Linda Myoki, *T'ai Chi as a Path of Wisdom*, Shambhala, Boston, 2001.

Leonard, Linda Schierse, *The Wounded Woman: Healing the Father–Daughter Relationship*, Shambhala, Boston, 1983.**

LeShan, Lawrence, *How to Meditate: A Guide to Self Discovery*, HarperCollins, New York, 1995.*

Levine, Stephen and Ondrea, *Who Dies? An Investigation of Conscious Living and Conscious Dying*, Random House, New York, 1982

Lewis, C.S., *Till We Have Faces*, Harcourt, New York, 1956.

——. *The Screwtape Letters*, Macmillan, New York, 1943.

Liebowitz, Judy and Bill Connington, *The Alexander Technique*, HarperCollins, New York, 1990.**

Liang, T. T., *T'ai Chi Ch'uan For Health and Self-Defense: Philosophy and Practice*, Vintage Books, New York, 1977.**

May, Rollo, *Power and Innocence: A Search for the Sources of Violence*, W.W. Norton, New York, 1998.**

Meister Eckhart: A Modern Translation, by Raymond Bernard Blakney, Harper & Brothers, New York, 1976.*

Merton, Thomas, *Contemplative Prayer*, Doubleday, New York, 1991.*

——. *No Man is an Island*, Harvest Books, New York, 2002.*

Moore, Thomas, *The Soul's Religion: Cultivating a Profoundly Spiritual Way of Life*, Perennial Classics, New York, 2003.**

O'Donohue, John, *Anam Cara: A Book of Celtic Wisdom*, HarperCollins, New York, 1997.*

Okakura, Kakuzo, *The Book of Tea*, Benjamin Press, Perryville KY, 2011.

Ortega y Gasset, Jose, *Man and People*, translated by Willard R. Trask, W.W. Norton, New York, 1957.

Ouspensky, P. D., *In Search of the Miraculous*, Harcourt, New York, 2001.**

Patanjali, *How to Know God: The Yoga Aphorisms of Patanjali*, translated with commentaries by Swami Prabhavananda and Christopher Isherwood, Vedanta Press, Hollywood CA, 1996.*

Pert, Dr. Candace, *Molecules of Emotion: The Science Behind Mind–Body Medicine*, Scribner, New York, 1997.

Prem, Sri Krishna, *The Yoga of the Bhagavad Gita*, Element Books, London, 1993.**

——. *The Yoga of the Kathopanishad*, J. M. Watkins, London, 1955.**

Ravindra, Ravi, *The Yoga of the Christ: In the Gospel According to St. John*, Element Books, Shaftesbury, UK, 1990.**

——. *Whispers from the Other Shore: A Spiritual Search – East and West*, Theosophical Publishing, Wheaton IL, 1984.*

Reps, Paul, *Zen Flesh, Zen Bones, A Collection of Zen and Pre-Zen Writings*, Charles Tuttle, Rutland VT, 1958.*

Reymond, Lizelle with Sri Anirvan, *To Live Within, A Woman's Spiritual Pilgrimage in a Himalayan Hermitage*, Rudra, Portland OR, 1995.**

Richards, M. C., *Centering, in Pottery, Poetry, and the Person*, Wesleyan University Press, Middletown CT, 1962.**

Rilke, Rainer Maria, *Letters to a Young Poet*, translated by M.D. Herter Norton, W.W. Norton, New York 2004.*

Rumi, Jalal al-Din, *The Essential Rumi*, translated by Coleman Barks, with John Moyne, A. J. Arberry and Reynold Nicholson, Castle Books, Edison NJ, 1997.**

Scaravelli, Vanda, *Awakening the Spine: A Stress-free New Yoga that Works with the Body to Restore Health, Vitality and Energy*, Harper San Francisco, 1991.**

Scholem, Gershom, *Major Trends in Jewish Mysticism*, Schocken Books, New York, 1995.

——. *Kabbalah*, Dorset Press, New York, 1987.

Schwaller de Lubicz, R. A., *The Temple in Man: The Secrets of Ancient Egypt*, Autumn Press, Brookline MA, 1977.**

The Secret of the Golden Flower: A Chinese Book of Life, translated into German by Richard Wilhelm, and from German to English by Cary F. Baynes, Harvest/HBJ Books, New York, 1970.

Shankara's Crest Jewel of Discrimination: Timeless Teachings on Nonduality, translated by Swami Prabhavananda and Christopher Isherwood, Vedanta Press, Hollywood CA, 1947.*

Siegel, Daniel, *Mindsight: The New Science of Personal Transformation*, Bantam Books, New York, 2011.**

Sloan, Carolyn, *Finding Your Voice: A Practical and Spiritual Approach to Singing and Living*, Hyperion, New York, 1999.**

Steinsaltz, Adin, *The Essential Talmud*, Basic Books, New York, 1984.

——. *The Thirteen Petalled Rose: A Discourse on the Essence of Jewish Existence and Belief*, Basic Books, New York, l985.*

Sun Tzu, *The Art of War*, Denma Translation Group, Shambhala, Boston, 2002.

Suzuki, D. T., *An Introduction to Zen Buddhism*, Grove Press, New York, 1991.

Suzuki, Shunryu, *Zen Mind, Beginner's Mind: Informal Talks on Zen Meditation and Practice*, Weatherhill Publishing, New York, l998.*

Tibetan Book of the Dead, translated by Robert Thurman, Bantam, New York, 1994.**

Tillich, Paul, *The Shaking of the Foundations*, Wipf & Stock, Eugene, OR, 2011.

——. *The Courage to Be*, Yale University Press, New Haven CT, 1952.

Trungpa, Chogyam, *Meditation in Action*, Shambala, Berkeley CA, 1970.*

Underhill, Evelyn, *Mysticism: A Study in the Nature and Development of Man's Spiritual Consciousness*, Dover Publications, New York, 2002.**

Upanishads: The Ten Principal Upanishads, translated by Shree Purohit Swami and William Butler Yeats, Faber and Faber, London, 1975.*

Vaysse, Jean, *Toward Awakening*, Far West Undertakings, San Francisco, 1978.**

Von Durckheim, Karlfried, *The Way of Transformation: Daily Life as Spiritual Exercise*, Allen & Unwin, London, l971.*

——. *Hara: The Vital Centre of Man*, Inner Traditions, Rochester VT, 2004.**

Weil, Simone, *Waiting for God*, Perennial Classics, New York, 2001.

Woodman, Marion, *Addiction to Perfection: The Still Unravished Bride*, Inner City Books, Toronto, 1982.**

——. *The Pregnant Virgin: A Process of Psychological Transformation*, Inner City Books, Toronto, 1985.**

——. *Leaving My Father's House: A Journey to Conscious Femininity*, with Kate Danson, Mary Hamilton and Rita Greer Allen, Shambhala, Boston, 1993.**

Woodman, Marion, with Robert Bly, *The Maiden King: The Reunion of Masculine and Feminine*, Owl Publishing, New York, 1999.**

Zweig, Connie and Jeremiah Abrams, editors, *Meeting the Shadow: The Hidden Power of the Dark Side of Human Nature*, Jeremy P. Tarcher, Los Angeles, 1991.

Yongey Mingyur Rinpoche, *The Joy of Living: Unlocking the Secret & Science of Happiness*, Three Rivers Press, New York, 2007.**

About the Author

PATTY DE LLOSA is a consulting editor of *Parabola* Magazine, a life coach and teacher of Tai Chi and the Alexander Technique in New York City. She has led group classes, daylong workshops and weeklong intensives in the Gurdjieff work, T'ai Chi, Qigong and Taoist meditation. Among her recent public venues are the New York Open Center, Wainwright House and the Lake Conference Center in New York State; Northern Pines Health Resort in Maine; the Peruvian Aikido Association in Lima, Peru; Columbia University Graduate Theater Program; the Society for Experimental Studies, Toronto. Her recently published articles appear in the Summer 2011 *Parabola* (The Neurobiology of WE), the Winter 2012 issue (Energy Therapy), Summer 2013 (Body Consciousness: Our Fundamental Power), Winter 2014 (From Bad to Good: You Can Get Here from There).

After graduating from Swarthmore College and a year at the Sorbonne, Patty worked as a reporter for *Time Magazine* for six years. She married a Peruvian and raised three children in Lima. When her husband became governor of Loreto province, she served as president of The Green Cross in Iquitos, supplying treatment and medicines to the needy in the Amazon jungle, and coordinating with the Peace Corps a summer visit of American doctors and young people to help build roads and schools. Returning to Lima, she founded and ran the first foreign chapter of the United Nations' pre-school, International Playgroup, for eight years.

When Patty returned to New York in 1979, she worked for six years as managing editor of *American Fabrics & Fashions Magazine*, moving on to become associate editor of Time Inc. startup *Leisure* and then deputy chief of reporters of *Fortune*. She retired in 1999 to take the three-year teacher-training program at the American Center for the Alexander Technique, while working halftime as communications director of internet startup e-academy, inc. and writing her first book: *The Practice of Presence: Five Paths for Daily Life* (Morning Light Press, 2006). Her second book is **Taming Your Inner Tyrant**: *A Path to Healing through Dialogues with Oneself* (A Spiritual Evolution Press, 2011). Both books are available in paperback and on Kindle and Nook.

Patty would love to hear from her readers at: patty@findingtimeforyourself.com.

Finis

En Theos (A God Within)

Now, Katherine, what do you mean by health? And what do you want it for?

Answer: By health I mean the power to live a full, adult, living, breathing life in close contact with what I love – the earth and the wonders there of the sea – the sun. All that we mean when we speak of the external world. I want to enter into it, to be part of it, to live in it, to learn from it, to lose all that is superficial and acquired in me and to become a conscious, direct human being. I want, by understanding myself, to understand others. I want to be all that I am capable of becoming so that I may be (and here I have stopped and waited and waited and it's no good — there's only one phrase that will do) a child of the sun. About helping others, about carrying a light and so on, it seems false to say a single word. Let it be at that. A child of the sun. Then I want to work. At what? I want so to work that I work with my hands and my feeling and my brain. I want a garden, a small house, grass, animals, books, pictures, music. And out of this, the expression of this, I want to be writing. (Though I may write about cabmen. That's no matter.)

But warm, eager, living life — to be rooted in life — to learn, to desire, to know, to feel, to think, to act. This is what I want. And nothing less. This is what I must try for.

From the *Journal of Katherine Mansfield*